Too Good
To Be True

"What a refreshing, honest, vulnerable presentation of the good news of God's grace, freely offered to all of us. Ricky's book is all the more special to me as I had a ringside seat watching my brother come alive to the only love that is better than life. Ricky writes less as a pastor and more as a fellow pilgrim in the heart-liberating journey to God's radical welcome for us in Jesus. Tired of holy hype and spiritual spin? Then this little gem is for you."

— DR. SCOTTY WARD SMITH
Teacher in Residence, West End Community Church, Nashville, TN

"Ricky is an infectious, wild, playful, honest, contagious carrier of this life he paints here so well. He weaves a compelling, modern-day explanation, defense and invitation of God. It all makes clear, winsome, profound and simple sense. The way the Gospel is supposed to look. He is exceedingly funny. And he is unsparingly honest about his pain, failure and loss. It makes you trust what he writes even more. My heart was deeply encouraged. I was reminded and drawn in again to the true and present love and life I have in Christ. Enjoy. This is the transforming, supernatural, grace-filled Gospel. It is for those of us who have forgotten, those beginning to wonder if it could be real, and for those of us who have given it out for decades and needed again to be encouraged it is all still true."

— JOHN LYNCH
Co-author of *The Cure* and author of *On My Worst Day*

Too Good To Be True

CHRISTIAN

HOPE

IN A

HOPELESS AGE

Ricky Jones

TOO GOOD TO BE TRUE
Christian Hope in a Hopeless Age

ISBN   978-1-61961-440-6 Paperback
        978-1-61961-441-3 Ebook

LIONCREST
PUBLISHING

ACKNOWLEDGEMENTS

I do not feel like I wrote this book as much as I remembered it. I remembered the teachings and illustrations that have been handed down to me from dozens of teachers and tried to copy them down in one place. Of those teachers I am the most thankful for the ones who invested time and energy into my life: Mark Maddox, Susan Gilroy, Jim Collier, Hal Farnsworth, Stan Weber, James Elkin, Duncan Rankin, Tim Starnes, and Fred Harrell. I hope I did you proud.

I would never have written this book without the encouragement and support of my friends, especially two families: the Halls and the Houstons. Thank you more than I can say. I do not deserve friends like you.

Thank you to everyone who supported me on Kickstarter, especially Brian Sorgenfrei, Wyatt Pickering, Christopher Key, Rick and Ann Hrechko, Scott Trew, Bryan and Stacie Gudgel, Dixon Williams, John and Rachel Brownlee, Isai Mireles, Kathy and Jim Crawford, Felix Belanger, and Emily and David Harbargar. This book would only be a good idea without you.

I want everyone to know I used a book writing service. I tried for two years to write this book but never got past the table of contents. A friend mentioned a book service called Book in a Box and I used them to complete the work. In the unlikely event that this book catapults me to celebrity status, I have already blown the whistle on myself.

Thank you RiverOaks Presbyterian Church for becoming the kind of community I always dreamed of, for loving me, and letting me write this book.

Finally, I wish I had the words to thank my wife appropriately but I don't. Any effort would sound cheesy and only fail to communicate a tenth of what I feel. Thank you, Bianca.

Contents

Preface

———————•———————

THE FIRST TIME I YELLED AT GOD, he chuckled. I was a freshman at Vanderbilt, and the year I enrolled, it had the wealthiest student body of any campus in the country. I studied there with people like Ross Perot's daughter and Roger Staubach's daughter. One guy on my hallway was a senator's son, and I felt like he was a king. I was a redneck from Dresden, Tennessee. My dad was a truck driver, and my mom ran the high school cafeteria. My going-away party was in a cow pasture. I showed up at Vanderbilt in my nicest pair of shoes, which were stained with cow manure. My T-shirt had "Rick the Lifeguard" airbrushed on it. Nothing about me fit in at Vanderbilt. I was extremely lonely.

That's not really why I yelled at God. That was part of it—I was sick of not having friends—but a bigger part of it was that family life had not worked out for me at all. My mom had been divorced once before she met my dad, and then my dad stopped coming home when I was in junior high. However, I kept praying that he would return. Some of my strongest religious memories were of being at prayer meetings as a fourth grader and fifth grader. When our whole church would meet together (there were only about twenty of us), I would stand up in front of the adults and beg for my dad to come home. Again and again, I pleaded that my dad would come home. He never did, and I was mad about that.

When I went to college, I was the good guy, the moral guy. I never got drunk until I was an adult. I never had sex. I was doing everything that I possibly could to be right, and it just wasn't helping at all.

So when my brother's wife asked him for a divorce, it felt like a tipping point. I started praying and fasting over and over. Every day I would fast for part of the day, through one meal at least, and beg the Lord to change their minds. He didn't. And when they got a divorce, I was just done. I went out into the middle of campus by myself and yelled at God. I said, "What good are you? If you can't save a marriage, what good are you?"

I felt scared because I was very serious. I was sick of it. I was done with God. I yelled, "I don't believe in you anymore!" And I swear, in the darkness, I felt him chuckle and say, "Then who are you talking to?"

I was frustrated, but I knew he was right. I thought, *Clearly, I do believe in you, 'cause I'm yelling at ya.*

At that point, I realized that peace wasn't going to be found by running away from him. I had to figure out who he was. So I started by giving more and more of myself to him. My sophomore year of college, I went to six Bible studies a week and prayer meetings at six-thirty in the morning. Every ministry on campus thought that I was their most committed student. I was trying to earn God's favor. I spent the summer between my freshman and sophomore year at a Christian camp. I loved it, but I couldn't go back there the next summer because I felt like those people were too rich and too white. And true Christians wouldn't work at a place like that. The next summer, I worked at an inner-city ministry, which was a disaster—I didn't have the patience for it, and I was far too intense. At one point, I threw a basketball at one of the kids, and I was screaming in his face because I wanted him to punch me. He didn't, of course. I was a total failure. I kept trying harder and harder, and I kept failing over and over. It became this pattern in my life.

This picture that haunted me was a picture of a Christian who had Jesus on the throne of his life, and all the dots of his life are in order. His life is settled. He has victory over sin. He wants to witness. He wants to pray. He wants to read his Bible. And that was just never, ever me. I wanted to study, I wanted to sleep, and I wanted to chase girls. I hated talking to people about Jesus. I'm still a terrible evangelist. I couldn't be what I was convinced that I ought to be, and the sin that I was committing never stopped or even slowed down. I would wake up every weekend in shame, thinking God was ashamed of me. I kept trying harder and harder, and finally I got sick of trying and wanted to quit.

Around that same time, Reformed University Fellowship came to Vanderbilt. I was one of the first students that the campus minister met with, and I very clearly remember telling him how burned out I was—how tired I was of trying to make God like me, how tired I was that I felt like I was the most Christian of all the people I knew and yet nothing really worked out for me. I was really pissed at my dad because he was trying to get back in my life like nothing had ever happened, and I didn't know what to do. I felt pressure to forgive him because it was the Christian thing to do, but I also kind of hated him. I had this inner battle going on, and I just dumped all this stuff on the minister. He listened and finally said, "Well, let me ask you this: you say you're the only Christian you know?"

I nodded, and he asked, "Why? Why are you the spiritual one?"

I didn't say anything. He said, "Let me ask you this: did any of your friends growing up go to church?"

I said, "Well, yeah, everybody I knew went to church."

He said, "Did any of them go to a better church than you went to?"

"Well, a lot of them did."

"Did any of them have better families than you?"

"Yeah, I'm the only one I know whose dad left."

"Then why are you Christian and they're not?"

At that point I was stuck because everything about me believed that the answer to that question was: I was better than they were. However, I knew that couldn't be the answer, right? The Bible says something about grace, I knew that much. But I didn't know what answer he was looking for, so I just didn't say anything.

The minister began to talk to me about grace. He said, "When your dad left, why didn't you go with him? What makes you so much better than him?"

I wanted so badly to get mad and yell. I wanted to defend myself and say, "Because I'm better than he is!" But that was just my pride speaking. I began to realize I was just as selfish as anyone—my selfishness just looked different. Instead of yelling, I began to learn about grace—that I did not earn God's concern for me. I did not make him start liking me. His love for me didn't start when I started doing good things. I loved him because he loved me first.

Grace began to make a difference. For the first time in my life, I had assurance of salvation. It was exciting. I felt loved and free for the first time. Yet I found that even though I had assurance of salvation, I was still very self-righteous and mean. God did not step in and fix me right away.

I went on to seminary and got my theology very precise. I came out of seminary well-intentioned, well-educated, and intolerable. As a youth minister while I was there, a group of students yelled at me to play *Dumb and Dumber*, and I responded by throwing their movie out of a moving bus. I was super right-wing in my theology and politics, and I thought, *If you don't agree with me, not only are you wrong, but you are also an idiot.*

Nonetheless, I still felt like I was gifted as a minister. I kept hearing how good I was and believing it—everyone always tells their preacher how good they are, and some of us actually believe it—and yet nothing was really happening in my ministry. People weren't really attracted to it or me.

For five years, I was a minister at Delta State University. I never had more than forty students really committed to the ministry, but I decided that I was too good to be there—which is odd, but arrogance is delusional. I started looking for jobs, and in a ten-month period I was turned down for thirteen jobs. With the first couple of rejections, you think, *Those guys are idiots! Can you believe they didn't hire me?* At some point you start to realize, *Maybe the problem is me?*

During that time, I was at a meeting at Independent Presbyterian in Memphis, and I was standing at a urinal next to my friend Jean Larroux. I was applying for a position as the campus minister at Auburn, and Jean asked if it looked like I was going to get the job. I said, "No, I couldn't even get an interview."

He said, "You know, that's too bad. You would've been a perfect campus minister there. It suits you perfectly. But you know what? When I first met you, you were a real jerk to me. You need to work on that."

I thought, *Well, that's an odd thing to hear at a urinal.* But I really took his words to heart. I started asking people how they perceived me, and I started praying to God to change things. As I did, I started to see things about myself that I didn't like: I wasn't very gentle, and I wasn't very kind.

One day, my wife Bianca, left me with our two boys, who were three and two at the time. We had a little courtyard where they could play and I could watch them from inside. While they entertained themselves, I was in my bedroom on my knees, praying that God would make me more gentle— praying over the fruits of the spirit. Suddenly, my child started crying and didn't stop. I got more and more annoyed that he wouldn't stop crying and that he was interrupting my prayers so that I could become a gentler person. It finally hit me how ironic that was, so I got up, opened the door, and found he had blood coming out the back of his head. He had fallen onto a drain and smacked his head, and I thought, *Great—I thought this was an abstract thing I was praying for, but I really am broken, and my selfishness is hurting the people I love.* I realized I needed to change.

Just because you realize something about yourself, does not mean you have the ability to change it. Soon after my realization, I went and talked to some campus minister buddies of mine and said, "Guys, am I the guy at the dinner table with barbecue sauce all over his chin, and no one has the courage to tell him to wipe it?" My friend Fritz Games said, "Ricky, you've got a chip on your shoulder so big nobody can get near you without knocking it off." It hurt.

That night was the second time I yelled at God. But this time I wasn't mad at him—I was mad at myself. I went to bed that night crying out, *Lord, you didn't die for me to leave me a jerk like this.* I started begging him to change me.

Soon after that, I listened to a sermon by Sinclair Ferguson where he said, "You treat other people exactly the way you believe God has treated you." I started thinking, *How do I believe God has treated me?* In my mind, God was the policeman in the rearview mirror—he didn't have his lights on, yet, but he was just waiting for me to do something wrong. He was just waiting. I was never good enough for him.

Sinclair talked about the goodness of God and believing it, and that really became a theme of my ministry. Once I realized I could trust God, that he cared for me, and I was precious to him, my ministry became more gentle and grace-filled. I started focusing on people who had grown up in the church but did not believe God was kind. I very clearly remember being in an empty football stadium with a student. She was crying and said, "You keep talking about the goodness of God, but the God I grew up believing in just wasn't good. He was just never happy with me. He was never satisfied." I took joy in teaching students that God was not only satisfied with them, but he was also thrilled with them.

I started working as a campus minister for Mississippi State and began to believe that God liked me. Although I was spending a lot of time healing broken people, I still felt unhappy with myself. I never thought I was doing enough. I had this drive and eventually left Mississippi State because the job became too easy. There was a kind of gnawing dissatisfaction inside of me that I had to be doing something harder or God wouldn't be pleased with me. And I wouldn't be pleased with myself.

I left Mississippi and threw myself into planting a church that didn't grow very quickly. It was difficult. But I was finally doing something hard enough for me. However, over and over, I was disappointed with myself, and I felt God was disappointed in me. I yelled at him for the third time, but this time, I wasn't yelling out because I was mad at him or even mad at myself. I was just crying, *I'm doing all I can do here, and it's not enough.*

Now living in Tulsa, I was becoming burned out again. During this time, while on a treadmill at the gym one afternoon, I had a vision. Now, I'm a Presbyterian, probably more Presbyterian than you. So if you're uncomfortable with visions, you can call it a daydream.

It was a Monday, and no one had come to church the day before. I had this vision of me coming off a football field having lost the game. Jesus was the coach, and I threw myself on his shoulder crying, and said, *I did everything I could. I tried as hard as I could.* The vision solidified what I believed about myself and the ministry: that I was never good enough for him.

Three weeks later I was on the treadmill again, and I had the same vision. But this time when I started crying on his shoulder saying, *I'm sorry, I'm so so sorry, I just couldn't do it,* Jesus took my head in his hands, looked me in the eye, and said, "Ricky, you're in the band; you're not on the team. I won the game. It's over. Your job is not to score touchdowns, and your job is not to win the game. Your job is to play the fight song to let everybody know that I won. Relax. The game is over. I've won it."

He began to show me that I had a completely false idea about what he wanted from me. I was trying so hard to earn forgiveness, to earn the death of Christ. I had a completely broken idea of what he was expecting of me, and he finally began to change that.

About six weeks after the second daydream, I had a third and final one (maybe Tulsa is a city of visions). Bianca and I had been on a date the night before, and it was beautiful.

At some point during that date, I looked at her and saw in her eyes how much she was enjoying having me there. As she smiled at me, I could tell I was making her as happy as she made me. The next day I got up, and as I was praying, God began to reveal to me that this is how he looks at me. Suddenly, scripture texts that I had said at least every week since I had become a minister began to make sense to me. All of a sudden, the lights came on: God is delighted with me.

Through this experience, God began to heal some very old scars. Ever since those dark days at college, I felt like no one really wanted me around, like I was a burden on people. The thought, the truth, that God—the creator of all things—likes me and is crazy about me and wants me around so much that he gave up his son for me overwhelmed me like a wrecking ball.

On Sundays at the end of church I say the benediction, "May the Lord bless you and keep you. May the Lord make his face to shine on you." Except I don't actually say those words because I say what they actually mean: "May the Lord make his face to smile upon you." That's what God wants for you to know—that he is smiling on you.

Or when I say, "The Lord your God is in your midst. He is mighty to save. He rejoices over you with gladness, he quiets you with his love, he celebrates over you with loud singing," I really mean, "He is delighted with you. You make him happy. He is happy to be alone with you."

Or this great one, which Jim Baird would say at the end of every worship service at First Presbyterian Church in Jackson, Mississippi: "Now unto him who is able to keep you from falling and to present you faultless before the presence of his glory with exceeding joy." That's not our joy. That text is saying that Jesus, when he presents you before the throne of God, will be giddy over you. *Look! We've got him here!* He is that delighted with you.

Or when Hebrews says, "Fix your eyes upon Jesus, the author and the finish of our faith, who for the joy set before him endured the cross." What motivated God to leave heaven to take on the form of a human, to suffer all the shame and the scorn of the cross, was the joy of having you. He is delighted in you.

When that was finally revealed to me, I thought it was too good to be true. That is pretty much the only thing I focus on now in my ministry, and I've written this book for people who grew up in the church but don't think God likes them. Based on my experience, I think there's a lot of you around. I want this book to find its way into every one of your hands and for you to realize that he is just giddy over you—in other words, he likes you.

CHAPTER I

The Spiral of Joy

"I am praying not only for these disciples but also for all who will ever believe in me through their message. I pray that they will all be one, just as you and I are one—as you are in me, Father, and I am in you. And may they be in us so that the world will believe you sent me...and that you love them as much as you love me. Father, I want these whom you have given me to be with me where I am."

— JOHN 17:20

WHEN THE BUZZER WENT OFF, I sprinted for the door. The cool thing about growing up in a small country town was that we were all free-range children. Our parents did not hover over us because we were always going to be seen by somebody who knew us. We could not be picked up by a stranger because no strangers ever visited our town.

My oldest brother's high school basketball team went to the state tournament in Nashville. And when the end-of-the-game buzzer sounded, I did what I always did in my hometown: I sprinted for the door. I took off for the parking lot alone, but it was so crowded that I couldn't get out. I was jostled and pushed in the crowd. I realized I was in a strange town and that there were a whole lot more people than I'd ever seen before. I felt terrified, realized I didn't even know where the parking lot was, and reached up to grab my mom's hand. Instead, I found myself holding the hand of a stranger. I'd left my mom behind, looked up at this stranger, and when she looked down at me, I was so terrified that I cried out. I took off running into the parking lot, looking around frantically, yelling for my mom. I was sure she had left me. Now was her chance to be rid of me forever.

I remember this big, older man—he seemed huge at the time—who stood four feet away from me. He saw I was lost, and even though he wasn't going to leave me, he wasn't going to get any closer either. He watched me as the cars kept emptying out of the parking lot, and I kept crying until I heard my mom's voice. She yelled my name, and I jumped up from where I sat, ran to her, and launched myself into her arms. She engulfed me in the best bear hug ever. In that hug, I felt warm, safe, loved, and most importantly, wanted. I was so happy that she had found me, and she was so happy that she had found me that we both started crying and laughing at the same time. Something deep inside me knew that I was making her happy. I think something inside of her knew that she was making me happy. It made me happy that I was making her happy, and it made her happy that she was making me happy.

Have you ever felt that way? I call that experience—one that I hope you've had at least once in your life—a spiral of joy. Simply knowing that a person is delighted with me makes me delighted with them. It's an upward spiral. These moments last only a few minutes, and they leave us longing for more.

I believe those moments of joy affect us so deeply because they reflect what has been going on in the heart of God forever. The Father and the Son have always been face to face. They have always been smiling on each other. The Holy Spirit has always been flowing between them. The three are so close together that it is impossible to distinguish where one ends and the other begins. The three are one, smiling on one another.

That experience, that spiral of delight, is an eternal reality at the foundation of creation. It is the very heartbeat of the image of God that you are created in. That's why those moments are so profound to us. That's why they resonate so deeply in our hearts.

Jesus describes his relationship with his Father by saying, "I was in you, and you were in me." It was a spiral of joy. Then he says, "I want these disciples to be with us because I want to be in them, so they can be in us and we can be in each other." I want you to hear that and think about this for a second.

Jesus says this prayer on the last night of his life. He starts the prayer off in John 17:1 by saying, "The hour has come." In the whole book of John, he has been saying, "This is not yet my hour. This is not yet my hour. This is not yet my hour. The hour is coming. The hour is coming." Finally he says, "The hour has come." He says, "This is it. I have done everything you have given me to do." In that intimate, extremely important prayer, where—let's be honest, he's going to get whatever he asks for—what does he ask? *He asks for you.* He says, "I want the people who are going to believe in me"— that's us—"I want them with me. I want them to be with me just like I am in you and you are in me. Not somewhere in heaven where I don't have to see them too often—I want them in me, I want to be face to face with them forever."

Please do not pass over this too quickly. Take a second and remember the deepest, most profound joy you have ever felt with another person. Remember the joy of your wedding day, the joy you felt when you held your baby for the first time, or a time when you came home from school crying and your mother met you with a warm hug. Now just imagine God, the creator of everything, feels that kind of joy for you. You make him that happy. More than anything else, he wants you to be with him.

Isn't that amazing? That's the heartbeat of the entire Bible. The Father, Son, and Holy Spirit, when they were contemplating creation, they saw that we were going to sin. They saw that we were going to ruin everything. And yet they thought we were worth it. Even though having us meant going through pain, misery, and sacrifice to save us, they wanted us. God would have to watch his image hurt and be hurt, abuse and be abused for centuries, but he still wanted us. He would take on human form and live a life of poverty and betrayal, ultimately arrested, tortured, shamed, spit upon, and killed. Even though it meant going through all of that, he thought we were worth it. He wanted to be with us that badly.

That's the beauty of the gospel and the heartbeat of the Bible. I want you to get this truth so deeply lodged in your heart that it becomes the standard you use to measure your own life. You are precious to God.

Do you feel that way? Or do you feel like God only likes you when you are doing everything right? I spent years trapped in anger and frustration, believing God was disappointed in me. I thought he hated the way I spoke, acted, and felt.

Nothing about me was good enough for him.

Most Christians think backward. We believe God is disappointed with us, tired of us, and sick of our constant requests and moral failures. Most of us interpret what God thinks about us based on how our lives are going. My team lost the football game. God must be mad at me. I failed a test. I must be doing something wrong. I don't have a girlfriend. *God, why are you mad at me?*

That's our inclination. But when you understand the Bible, the gospel stands all of that on its head. We're able to say, "The Lord, who loves me so much he gave his only son for me, didn't think I needed to pass that test." Or, "He didn't want me to have that girlfriend." That gives us peace and the ability to life live. I don't know what you're going through or why you are going through it, but I know why it's not—you are not suffering because God doesn't love you. It can't be that.

One of my good friends is a golf pro and instructor. In 2015, he signed on to personally coach one of the top pros in the world. Under his tutelage, that golfer went from being ranked the seventy-eighth in the world to the twelfth. My friend received more coaching contracts, and it looked like he had finally made it. We were so pumped. He had been working his tail off for years, and he finally made it because he signed this huge client. Three weeks before the Masters, his client fired him. My friend called me from the airport, and I asked how he was doing. He said, "That's twenty-five thousand dollars I'm not going to make this year." He said, "I'm disappointed, but I know it's not because Jesus doesn't love me. It can't be that. It just can't be that."

That's the perspective I want you to see life through. Life's hard. It's not a romantic comedy that always has a happy ending. But whatever happens, it is not because God doesn't love you. It can't be that.

• How is our ministry different if we really believe this?

Look at the joy on the bride and groom's faces.
Jesus looks at you with the same look of delight.
Is that too good to be true?

CHAPTER II

The Spiral of Shame

———————●———————

"*The Lord observed the extent of human wickedness on the earth, and he saw that everything they thought or imagined was consistently and totally evil. So the Lord was sorry he had ever made them and put them on the earth. It broke his heart.*"

—GENESIS 6:5–6

Broken idols, broken heads
People sleeping in broken beds
Ain't no use jiving
Ain't no use joking
Everything is broken

—BOB DYLAN, "EVERYTHING IS BROKEN"

AN ARMY RANGER WALKED the fluorescent-lit aisles of a convention center, passing rows and rows of displays. Finished with the army, he looked to the ministry as a possible new career path, and the conference offered seminars, panels, and discussions on life and work in the church. Tables set up by various ministries held pamphlets and information cards. One display by a ministry for racial reconciliation and justice stood out. On the table was a picture of a young African in chains, eyes staring straight out at him.

The picture was so striking that the ranger began to weep. He felt the pain, the evil, and the brokenness of the world, and in the middle of the carpeted convention center, he wept. A black woman rose from the table, approached him, and embraced him. As she held him, she whispered in his ear, "It's not supposed to be this way, is it, honey?"

He cried and said, "It's not supposed to be this way. It's not supposed to be this way. It's not supposed to be this way." She replied, "Jesus is going to make it all right. Jesus is going to make it all right."

Each of us has experienced a moment where we thought, *It's not supposed to be this way.* Maybe it was the loss of a loved one, the end of a marriage, the loss of a house, or the news of a major, or even minor, catastrophe. Death, heartbreak, and divorce have all found us at this place, and from some angles, it seems the world is broken. At its worst, it's abusive. We see and hear of children and spouses abused by loved ones and caregivers. We see wars and crimes. We see broken relationships. We see mothers and fathers leaving their children, and children who have to be one person with their mother on the weekend, and another person with their father the next. We see children who do not know who they are and who are not given a chance to develop as a person.

This world is broken because we are broken. God created us for a relationship with himself. When we are not in that relationship, we feel a void, a crippling hole inside us that leaves us longing for more than this life can give. Some people manipulate others to try to force them to fill that void, while others turn on themselves.

We see extreme levels of self-hatred—people practicing self-mutilation, cutting themselves, or just thinking abusive thoughts as they view themselves in the mirror. One man I knew—a guy I would trade bodies with in a second—was a Division-I football player at a university. He is the strongest man I've known. He told me he was convinced that if he ever got fat, his wife would leave him. He works out two hours a day because he's dissatisfied with his body. He's afraid that if he doesn't exercise, he won't be loved by someone he loves.

When we see those who seem to have it good thinking they

have it bad, we think, *It's not supposed to be this way*. In a 2005 interview for *60 Minutes*, Tom Brady said, "Why do I have three Super Bowl rings and still think there's something greater out there for me? I mean, maybe a lot of people would say, 'Hey, man, this is what it is.' I've reached my goal, my dream, my life. Me, I think, 'God, it's gotta be more than this.'" Brady was only twenty-eight years old at the time, and it seems fitting that he indirectly addresses God in that statement. When the interviewer asked what he thought that something more might be, Brady answered, "I wish I knew."

If I told you "Good looks will never be enough," you might respond, "How would you know?" If I said, "The perfect girlfriend or boyfriend will never satisfy you," you might answer, "You wouldn't know." If I said, "There's no amount of money in the bank that could make you happy," you might reply, "Prove it."

But when NFL quarterback Tom Brady expresses that he feels a sense of lack, even after multiple Super Bowl trophies and MVPs and millions in the bank, we don't believe him. We think, *What could possibly be good enough?* We think, *It's not supposed to be this way*. If someone who has everything tells you it's not enough, that testifies to our emptiness, and how we are created for something more.

Nothing in this world can fill that void. Adam and Eve, our first parents, like every person since then, turned away from God. We don't let him fill us. We don't trust him to fill us. We don't want to be known by his embrace. We don't want to know ourselves deeply or be defined by this relationship of being loved. Yet we're at home and in joy when we are in that embrace.

I have four boys, all teenagers now. When the youngest was four, we were walking back to the house when he took off running and yelled, "Race you home!" He was way ahead of everyone else, and the eldest, my eight-year-old, sprinted to catch up. He could not imagine losing this race to his brother, who was half his age. He ran as fast as he could, and right before his brother reached the driveway, the eldest grabbed him and pulled him to the ground. When I caught up to them, I said, "Son, you've got to believe that you're not important because you're fast. You've got to believe that you're important because I love you."

He did not want to be defined by my love for him, by our relationship. He wanted to be known for his own achievement. We all act the same way toward God.

By far, the most important thing that could be said about you is that the creator of everything knows you and loves you. You are precious to him. There is nothing you can achieve that will be bigger than that. We're going to be empty until we let our relationship define us. And until we let this fill us, we will feel the void of shame and guilt.

After thirteen years in the ministry, my faith was tested by the death of my brother. Two wreckers pulled at the car in opposite directions, as it had to be completely ripped apart to get him out, As I stared at the wreckage, I thought, *That's appropriate. My life has just been ripped open.*

Until you've buried someone you love, you just don't know— or don't feel, or don't want to feel—the meaninglessness of life. Nothing matters in this life if death ends it. At the moment of my brother's death, I felt that crippling void, that cry from within, *It's not supposed to be this way. It's not supposed to be this way.* Acknowledging this void and asking *why* poses the question that our faith in God can answer.

We try to cover our feelings of shame, insecurity, and unworthiness with cloaks. We try to fill the void. Some of us fill it with long hours at work, with success, and with the aim of being the absolute best, while others fill it with religion, with being good, and with trying to serve other people. Still others try to stop up that void, numbing it, by never thinking about anything beyond the next party, the next paycheck, the next drink, the next hit, the next high, the next big purchase, the next vacation, or the next sexual partner. Many are trying not to think about it, but nobody escapes it. We seek to know ourselves independently from God and leave ourselves feeling insecure and unfulfilled. You can't fill it on your own. As Cher used to sing, "We all sleep alone, and you always wake up by yourself."

Centuries ago, Saint Augustine said, "You made us for yourself, and we will always be restless until we find our rest in thee."[1]

If Tom Brady, Cher, and St. Augustine are essentially saying the same things, albeit from very different spectrums of time and place, then we can agree we're onto something here.

Saint Augustine's path to Christianity was tumultuous at best. In his autobiography, *Confessions*, he writes of stealing fruit not because he was hungry, but because it was not allowed, and as an adolescent, he lived a life of hedonism, eventually trading wanton sexual immorality with a life of scholarship. None of it was good enough, not even the life of a scholar, and none of it was fulfilling until he surrendered to Christ and received him. Even though Saint Augustine was born in 354, his experience speaks to our contemporary culture and the wanton sexual immorality: we're longing for this embrace, but we never turn to God

---

1 Saint Augustine. "Confessions," *Book One.*

to receive it. It takes us so long to come to our senses and say, "Maybe I'm trying to get filled with something that's not going to do it." Instead, we think, *Maybe if it were more, more, more, then maybe that would do it*. We have to realize that we're eating the wrong thing. Yet we'll try everything and anything because we know it's not supposed to be that way.

Sometimes, that means trying really hard to be good. In college, I awoke at six every morning and attended five Bible studies a week, plus prayer meetings. All it ever did was cover me with even more guilt because I wasn't everything I thought I ought to be. One summer, I worked at Christian camp and felt guilty about it because I thought I wasted my summer trying to help rich kids. So the next summer, I signed up to help poor kids, which was a disaster. I desperately wanted those kids to love me, to see my sacrifice for them, and to appreciate me. I didn't know it at the time, but I was just using them to fill that void in my heart. Once when I saw how little they respected me, I got so angry that I threw a basketball at one of the kids. The true nature of my service was revealed: I was there only for myself.

The more I tried to do, the more I saw that I wasn't doing. I was like that body builder—the stronger I became, the more I saw my weaknesses. I was left with a greater sense of unworthiness, unable to fill it.

This is what I mean when I say we're seeking to know ourselves independently from God. I tried to do it all on my own: volunteering, studying, waking up early, and taking on more, more, and more. Whether it was good deeds or bad, the fact that I was doing it alone meant it was never going to get me where I wanted to be—it was only going to make me feel my independence, my emptiness.

One of the first things I tell those who go into the ministry is, "God doesn't need you." It sounds harsh, but until we figure that out, we're never going to be at peace. God doesn't need us for anything. And yet, there is a lot of hubris in the Christian community. The message is, "Go out and do great things for God." But he doesn't need us. He already likes us—he loves us. Until we understand that, there is no joy or peace to be found.

This is an extremely difficult concept, but the most valuable things in my life have not been earned, as we're taught in our culture. The most valuable things in my life—the love of my mother, the love of my brothers, the love of my spouse—are not earned but received.

To fill this void, we must stop running away from God. We need to stop and let him fill us.

Oliver was four years old, chasing his older sisters around the house. They had adopted the role of mothering him while their parents were occupied, and he was pretty tired of it. So as he ran in circles, he held a rock in his right hand. Remember, he was four years old, and when he threw the rock, there was very little chance he'd hit them. He launched it in their direction, and it missed the girls, going nowhere near them. However, it did go straight into the family's brand-new flat-screen television.

The whole house stood in dreadful silence. His sister looked down at Oliver and said, "Oh, Oliver, you're going to get it when Daddy gets home." Oliver, stunned with fear and disbelief, terrified because he knew he did something he wasn't supposed to do and his father was going to be so disappointed, cried and cried and cried. Fearing what his family would say, Oliver hid.

When his father came home and found him, he asked Oliver what was wrong. Oliver, still crying, told his father what had happened. His father embraced him and said, "Son, I love you so much more than I love this television."

That's the irony of life: the only person who can fix this mess or mistake is the person who bought the television, and the only person who can make Oliver feel better is his father, whom Oliver is scared of and runs away from. It's easy to get caught in another kind of spiral: the spiral of feeling like a failure, a spiral of shame. When we're in this place, we run *from* God instead of *to* him. We try harder to fill that gap, and the harder we try to fill it, the more we feel the emptiness and the harder we run away, thus we enter a spiral of unworthiness, shame, and fear.

When Dean Smith was coaching basketball at North Carolina, a student and player who was in trouble with the law disappeared for weeks. The student sneaked into Smith's office one day, and when Smith saw him, he locked the door, trapping the student there. He turned to him and asked, "Why have you been running away from me? Don't you know I am the only person in this city who can help you?"

Our guilt and unworthiness make us want to run away from God. When I mentioned how, in college, I felt like God was the policeman in the rearview mirror, waiting for a reason to turn his lights on, what I did not—could not—realize at that age was that he was there to help and that he was the only one able to help me.

But we don't want to run to God. We do not think we can trust him. After all, he is responsible for all of this brokenness, right? If he is so good, why doesn't he just make it better? Can we trust him?

About a year ago, my wife and I got in a huge fight, where the particulars are not as important as the fact that I was absolutely convinced that I was right and she was wrong. I was so looking forward to her coming home so she could apologize to me that I rehearsed in my mind how magnanimous I would be. I had this whole big speech planned where I would forgive her. She did not see it that way. Instead of "forgiving her," I ended up apologizing and making an appointment with my marriage counselor.

The session was completely focused on me. I had wildly overreacted to something she had said, to which the counselor responded, "When we overreact, there's something in our past that we haven't dealt with. It's like when you come home from work and you kick the dog. Why do you kick your dog when he has not done anything? You kick your dog because you can't kick your boss. You can kick the dog, but you can't kick your boss."

I was forced to confront all of my unresolved issues with my father. The counselor said, "You have a lot of energy in your body, so don't try to work this out by journaling or doing any of those things. You need to go out into the woods and throw rocks and hit trees." So I did. I spent a full day in the woods, throwing things, kicking things, and having an honest conversation with God. I ran right up to him and said, "You knew what my dad was going to be like, and you didn't stop him!" I heaved a rock at a tree trunk, and it flew off into a pile of leaves.

"He shouldn't have done what he did. If I saw someone doing something wrong, and I could have stopped him, I would. I'm angry that you didn't stop him."

God's responses were all in agreement, which can be annoying when you want to pick a fight with someone. He said, "I get it. What do you want to do?"

I said, "I want to hit you. I wish you would come down here so I could hit you."

He said, "OK. What else?"

I said, "I want to yell at you."

God responded, "If I came down there, would you yell at me?"

"Yeah!"

"Would you beat me?"

"Yeah!"

"Would you spit on me?"

"Yeah!"

God said, "I've done all that for you. I came as a man. You think your family is a problem? My family betrayed me. My family abandoned me. They thought I was crazy. They tried to end my ministry. You think you have problems with money? I was homeless, had no place to lay my head. You think you have problems with friends? One of my twelve closest friends sold me for thirty pieces of silver. You think you have problems with shame? I was stripped naked and laughed at and mocked for hours. You think you have problems with injustice? Three times I was declared completely innocent and then I was executed for my innocence."

He continued, "I know the world is broken, and I know you want to beat me up for it. I want you to know that I have suffered for it."

I never expected an answer like that. I had never really thought about how this broken world had hurt God more than it hurt me. In those woods, I realized God was not distant and uninvolved. He had not abandoned me to be hurt while he wasn't looking. I started crying, at first angry tears of self-pity, but they changed to tears of contentment. I realized I could trust God even with this broken world and my broken heart.

When we get mad, we view God and Christ as living up on a mountain, smiling over everything that happens on earth.

Without the incarnation, we have no sense of how Christ has suffered for the brokenness of this world. He became man so he could suffer for it. He was beaten and killed for that brokenness, even though he was not at fault. He experienced everything he has called us to experience. And by his experience, he has begun the healing process.

CHAPTER III

The Lender Pays the Debt

———•———

"And forgive us our debts, as we also have forgiven our debtors."

—MATTHEW 6:12

Will you forget when we have paid our debts,
Who did we borrow from? Who did we borrow from?
—THE AVETT BROTHERS, "THE PERFECT SPACE"

CENTURIES AGO, in ancient China, there was a well in the center of a town. During yearly droughts, the town enforced strict water rations, and anyone caught stealing water was beaten. One searing summer afternoon, the town's bailiff arrived at the judge's office with news that someone was apprehended at the well. The judge asked the bailiff why he looked so sad to deliver the news. The bailiff said, "You'll see."

Outside at the well, the judge saw his own mother, sick with a fever, guarding a bucket of stolen water.

On the one hand, the judge loved his mother and felt compassion toward her. On the other hand, the judge knew that if he made one single exception, the whole town would crumble. Lawlessness would prevail, riots would break out around the well, the town would run out of water, and everyone would die. He knew that to be seen as just, he had to convict his mother. He said, "You've committed a crime," and sentenced her to corporeal punishment: forty blows in the center of town while tied to a stake.

The mother was brought to the square, and when she was tied to the stake, the judge removed his own robes, embraced his mother, turned to the bailiff, and said, "Make sure every blow falls on my back." In this way, the judge is still just—ensuring every crime is punished to the full extent of the law—while also being loving—taking the punishment on himself.

I've already mentioned how God created us to be in a relationship with him that feels like a spiral of joy, and still we continue to look for joy on our own. Rejecting him has left us feeling a void that nothing on earth can fill, and God has allowed us to feel that void so that we would ultimately turn back and embrace him. To understand this, we have to look at how God has removed every obstacle between us and him so that we may enter into his joy.

The first obstacle is our sin, which the Bible uses several metaphors to describe—disease, death, slavery, lawlessness, and debt. In this chapter, I will refer to our sin as debt, which we can run up in two ways: first, we could fail to pay someone something that we rightfully owe. Second, as Oliver in the previous chapter could tell you, we can break something that belongs to someone else. When it comes to our relationship with God, we have done both.

At the heart of the gospel is the amazing news that God has taken that debt on himself by giving us his only son. In 2 Corinthians 5:20-21, it reads, "God made him who knew no sin to be sin for us so that we might become the righteousness of God."

God is the judge who embraces us and takes our punishment upon himself. Modern critiques of the historic gospel often foolishly say that the father is punishing the son—some kind of divine child abuse—which misses the fact there is only one God. He is the Father, Son, and Holy Spirit. He is taking the punishment for the sins that he forgives.

Our culture often talks about debt, from national debt to personal debt or home mortgages, and it seems that everybody has the thought of it in the back of their minds. The recession of 2008 drove many individuals, corporations, and even some nations into debts they could never repay—numbers most of us cannot fathom. This realization cast many borrowers into anxiety and even despair. The debt no longer felt like a harmless cloud hanging over their heads, threatening rain, but more like a bulldozer revving its engines menacingly. Finding a way out felt impossible, because only the lender had the authority to cancel our debts.

The Bible describes our sin as our debt to God; therefore, he alone can forgive it. The weight of our sins causes some people to fear and run from him, but the Bible tells us a reassuring truth: that God himself has paid the exorbitant price we owe. He has forgiven our debts. Not only this, but he has also shared his wealth with us, a wealth greater than any here on earth.

Where does this debt come from? First, we have not been who we ought to have been, and have not loved God the way he deserved. God is not some far-off distant ideal. He is personal and involved with your life. You owe your existence to him. It's akin to how we feel toward our mothers—how, no matter how often you call or how many things you do for her, it never feels like it's enough. How do you pay back the person who brought you into the world, raised you, sacrificed her life for you, dressed you, fed you, and protected you?

The debt to God is real in that way. He sustains our existence, he loves us, and he creates us. We owe him our joy, love, obedience, and affection, and not giving that to him breeds this feeling of unworthiness. There's the debt—the things we should do that we haven't done.

Then there is also the second way we build debt—or guilt—and the things that we did that we should not have done. Turning away from him to find something else to fulfill us only increases the debt, as he alone deserves our adoration and trust. When we search for something else and trust in that to make us whole, we are essentially committing a kind of adultery—giving the love that only he deserves to something or someone else.

Then there are our transgressions—the hurtful things we have done or said to others ignite a righteous anger in God, the loving father who feels protective of his children. Yet God is not vindictive or mean. His anger is like that of a father, and everyone on this planet is his son or daughter. Everything that is done to them—every lie that is told about them, every blow that they're struck with, every individual who is molested or taken advantage of—is heard and felt by him. He feels this protective anger fueled by his love for us.

We live in a weird time, where we can watch the news as much or as little as we want, and at some point, we all say, "That's it. I can't stand it anymore." We turn off the news and go about our day. We look away. We stop bearing witness, whereas God never looks away. He sees everything and sees it for what it really is. When someone views pornography and fantasizes about the beautiful woman on-screen, God sees the girl who was sexually abused as a child, whose sense of self-worth is wrapped up in exterior looks, who has been mistreated her whole life. There's no false glamour here, only the truth.

God is angry that his children get hurt. It's a righteous anger. Every hurtful word, thought, or action against one of his children hurts him. It is like we are breaking every TV in his house. We just keep building up that debt. We feel it—we feel left in this gap of being separated from him, unable to pay the debt, and feeling guilty. God pays the price for the sins we commit against him. He is the compassionate judge, and our debts to him are so huge that we are unable to pay them, and we know that he's the only one who could. We are guilty, and we know it. Still, he takes the punishment for our sins on himself. He comes to us having done everything necessary to pay our debt, even providing his son, a painful sacrifice made because of his great love for us.

We're told in the gospels that the night before Jesus went to the cross, he went out into a garden with those closest to him and begged them to pray for him. He did not want to be alone and was so overwhelmed with anxiety, experiencing a terrifying dread greater than any felt by man before or since. He sweat blood, asked his friends to stay awake and pray with him, fell to the ground and pleaded with his father to save him from the cross because he knew the terror he was about to face.

The Bible describes the death of believers as falling asleep and passing into new life, but Jesus understood that his death would be a personal holocaust. He knew that God's arms would not be open wide when he faced the Father dressed in our sin. God would be armed with all of his holy hatred of sin. To free his children from punishment and bring them into new life, God would have to pour all of his wrath out on the body of his son. Jesus faced death feeling terrified, and he did this for us. He didn't know all that was coming, but he faced it willingly. He faced utter darkness, abandonment, emotional pain, and deep physical pain all out of love for his father and out of a longing to be with us. There is no greater love than this.

If you are a parent, you know the pain of watching your child suffer, whether he has a small cold or a full-blown illness. You may have even heard the saying, "You will only be as happy as your least happy child." Our hearts are tied to our children's lives. When they suffer, we suffer. Jesus, God's son, was not the only one offering his life as a painful sacrifice at the cross. His holy Father was giving up his beloved son for us in an act of extravagant grace. This act would cause him bitter pain, and he suffered it because he wanted us to be with him.

I know you have probably heard all this before, but take a minute to weigh it in your mind. God, who is perfectly holy and loving, should never have to feel pain or loss. Yet he willingly suffered to pay the debts we owed him. He suffered for what we have done because he wants to be with us. If you saw someone do that in a human context, you would never believe it. You would say it was too good to be true.

Imagine a scenario: Some people read this book and feel like it was a complete waste of their time. In the middle of the night, they awake full of rage and drive all the way to Tulsa to tell me off. When they reach my house, they decide to burn it down. The fire department arrives, the police arrive, and they are arrested. A judge declares the bail will be $500,000. At the station, when the authorities grant them one local phone call, they realize the only person they know in Tulsa is me. So they call me, and I drive over and can't help but laugh at these people sitting in a jail cell for burning down my house and then calling me to help them out. They see me and say, "I know this is unconventional, given that we've just burned down your house, but could you pay our bail?" To which I would respond, "No, because (a) I don't really know you and don't like you, (b) you burned down my house, and (c) I don't have half a million dollars."

Then they say, "We're from California, and we know some real wicked people. We know someone who would pay real good money for a teenage boy. Could you sell your thirteen-year-old son into slavery to get us out of jail for burning down your house?"

It's so absurd that one may have to read that paragraph a few times to understand the flawed logic. That's asinine, right? No one in his right mind would ever sell his thirteen-year-old son to pay bail for someone who just burned down his house.

Yet this is the extravagant grace that we're confronted with in the gospel—that God gave his son to the cross to forgive us for sinning against him, to forgive a debt we couldn't pay. The judge embraces the defendant and the blows fall on his own back. It sounds believable when we tell it as a legend set in ancient China, but when we are taught that God sacrificed Jesus on the cross as a way to reconcile us to him, we think it's too good to be true.

CHAPTER IV

A Living Savior

———————•———————

"For I delivered to you as of first importance what I also received: that Christ died for our sins in accordance with the Scriptures, that he was buried, that he was raised on the third day in accordance with the Scriptures, and that he appeared to Cephas, then to the twelve. Then he appeared to more than five hundred brothers at one time, most of whom are still alive, though some have fallen asleep."

—1 CORINTHIANS 15:3–6

ON THE THURSDAY BEFORE HIS DEATH, Jesus ate his last meal with the disciples, and one whispered, "Who is it that is going to betray you?" Jesus said, "The person I give this piece of bread to will be my betrayer." He dipped a piece of bread into a cup and handed it to Judas. When Judas took it, Satan entered into him, and Jesus looked him in the eye and said, "What you're about to do, do it quickly."

Isn't that stirring? Satan entered Judas, and Jesus, in modern-day terms, said, "Bring it on, and do it now." Judas slipped out into the darkness, and Satan began his attack. He lulled Jesus's friends to sleep, and sent terror, anxiety, and loneliness his way. Jesus alone withstood it and did not break. Satan returned with betrayal, arrest, and abandonment, but Jesus willingly submitted to the soldiers so that his friends might go in peace. Satan attacked with injustice, lies, and accusations, but Jesus did not falter. Jesus was beaten, shamed, mocked, and stripped, but not broken. Finally, Satan poured death upon him, and Jesus swallowed that death.

God wants to live with us in a spiral of joy, yet we tried to create our own joy independently of him and have failed miserably. Still, he invites us back into relationship with him, and removes the obstacle of our sin so we can come home. Now we see that God is not content to only embrace us for a little while. He wants to embrace us forever, so he needs to remove the obstacle of death, which Jesus defeated at the resurrection.

We are told that Jesus laid down his life on his own. "No one takes my life from me, but I lay it down of my own accord" (John 10:18). He willingly went to the cross and perished. And when his body was entombed, the grave tried to hold him. However, the grave trying to hold Jesus was like a single lightbulb trying to contain the power of an entire nuclear reactor. His power was too great, and Jesus exploded the grave from within. "God raised Jesus from the dead, freeing him from the agony of death, because it was impossible for death to keep its hold on him" (Acts 2:24).

When he did that, he put an end to evil as the last word. Evil would not be the last word, darkness would not be the last word, and sickness would not be the last word because death would not be the last word. Life and hope would go on forever, be eternal, because Jesus had won.

That is what Easter is. Easter is a message that our shame, our guilt, and our sin have been removed; that Jesus has the receipt, and he paid the debt in full. It is our message of victory over everything that threatens to undo us. It says Jesus has defeated the cancer that leaves us all so desperately broken, and he will walk with us down the path toward healing. God has committed everything he has to our redemption and will not give up on us until we are with him and like him in glory.

Easter has become the last of a string of holidays, following Christmas, New Year's, and Valentine's Day. We break out our white shoes and pink ties, go to church, and watch the Masters golf tournament. We tend to treat Easter like the forgotten stepchild of the holidays, but Easter holds more weight than the rest. Without the resurrection, every act of love toward another person would be wasted when she dies.

Because of the resurrection, every kind act toward another person lives on and matters forever. The resurrection is what separates Jesus from everyone else who has ever set foot on this earth, separates him from other religious leaders, and separates Christianity from all other religions.

The resurrection is the victory—the message that Jesus did not lose, that he overwhelmed our shame and our sin, that he confronted and defeated pain, betrayal, injustice, and death. This, in many ways, is the center point of Christianity. Most importantly, Easter is true.

One spring, I was invited to preach at a conference, and as I prepared to speak to eight hundred college kids, someone asked me, "What are you preaching on?" That's just about the worst question one could ask an introvert, as I was so afraid he'd think it was a stupid idea, and I had no time to change the topic. I took a deep breath and told him, "I'll be talking about the resurrection." The man proceeded to tell me about the woman he brought with him as a guest—her brother had committed suicide two months prior. He talked with her a lot about the resurrection recently, and I said, "The older I get, the more I realize it is the only thing that matters." To which he replied, "If the resurrection isn't true, Christianity is simply a bunch of bedtime stories—absolutely worthless."

I didn't fully understand this until thirteen years into my

work as a minister. In August 2008, my brother was in a horrific car accident. After he was extracted from the vehicle with the Jaws of Life, doctors were not able to save him. He was forty-six years old. As his coffin was lowered into his grave, I thought, *Either I believe that I'm going to see my brother again or I don't.*

I've never been at a place where I actively, intentionally did not believe in the resurrection, but it was not something that I focused on. If someone asked if I believed in the resurrection, I said yes without hesitation. However, I was mostly interested in and occupied by other topics: the incarnation, God's existence, justification, and sanctification. Yet the resurrection is such a cornerstone of Christianity that one can't say one doubts it and work as a minister. However, when I came to a point where I had to put my hope in the resurrection, my faith failed me. I just did not believe it.

I encourage people to doubt whether they actually believe it. Typically, folks have a very traditional faith in the resurrection, accepting it because their family did—they believe in it because their family did in the same way they root for the hometown football team because their family did. There's nothing real or weighty to it, nothing life-transforming about it—it's just there. I often challenge others not to accept something handed down to them but to ask themselves, "Do I believe it?"

That's what I asked myself as my brother was lowered into his resting place. And the answer wasn't an immediate, emphatic yes but more like, "I'm not sure I really believe this, and I need to know."

I know I am not alone because when I interview people who join the church, they seldom, if ever, mention the resurrection. I ask them what they believe, and they often say, "I believe in Jesus."

"Great," I reply, "what about him?"

"He's the Son of God," is the usual response, to which I ask, "What else?"

"He died for our sins."

I say, "Great. So far so good. What else?" This is the point in the conversation where the replies become less sure: "Um, he likes us? He hears our prayers?"

"Do you pray to Jesus?" I ask. People nod and say yes. This is where I really start to fish for answers. "So, you said Jesus died for our sins. Why do you pray to someone who is dead?" People stop and think for a moment before saying, "Because he was raised from the dead." Even those who are not clear on the specifics of Christianity understand that Jesus was resurrected.

Still, I needed to know why I believed in it. Even though I encouraged others to question their traditional beliefs, I hadn't given myself the same opportunity.

I faced my doubts and fears head-on, throwing myself into the resurrection, studying and examining the Bible. What first struck me was how it was written for people who did not believe in it. This is important, given that we often look back with a kind of chronological snobbery and think, *This happened thousands of years ago, when people believed in things like resurrections.* Except that they didn't. No one expected or believed in a resurrection—a pretty central and ingrained fact of human history was that people who died remained dead.

None of the disciples or followers of Jesus even thought he would be raised from the dead, despite Jesus telling them so. Even though they were told, no one was there to bear witness. I don't know about you, but if someone told me they were going to rise from the dead in a few days, I would be first in line to see it. The first people to find Jesus did not believe what had happened. They had to be convinced, and he had to keep appearing to them.

Luke, in Acts 1, says: "We are told everything about Jesus, everything that Jesus began to do and teach until the day he was taken up to Heaven after giving his chosen apostles further instructions. During the forty days after his crucifixion, he appeared to the apostles from time to time and he proved to them in many ways that he was actually alive, and he talked to them about the kingdom of God."

This description was written for those who did not believe—the skeptics. It's described by authors who didn't expect it, had come to believe it, and wanted to explain why or how to other readers. Jesus kept returning to prove that he was alive. Those who saw him crucified thought—and rightly so—he had died. If you watched a friend die, and he returned to tell you he was still alive, you would probably think it was some sick and elaborate practical joke, a nightmare, or an episode of a bad reality television show.

Jesus appeared again and again, doing concrete things with his disciples. He cooked meals for them, broke bread with them, and ate with them. He looked at them and said, "Do not be afraid." He said, "A spirit doesn't have flesh and blood even as I have." And still, they were flustered, shocked, and unbelieving—pretty much what you would expect to read in a historically accurate account. In spite of this, Jesus remained gracious with them. They doubted him, and he listened to those doubts. If you grow up in the church, you may be familiar with the term *doubting Thomas*, which refers to the Apostle Thomas, who said to Jesus that he wouldn't be fooled. Rather than scold him or become angry,

Jesus encouraged Thomas to try to believe. He said, "Believe. I am real."

It would have been easy to chalk it all up to a mass hallucination. However, the tomb was empty. Peter stood in front of a thousand people on Pentecost—in front of those who had put Jesus to death and watched him die only forty days prior—and said, "Go look at the tomb. It's empty. He is not there" (Acts 2:32).

Still, I thought, the disciples could have made all of this up— one elaborate lie. Right? Maybe they designed an elaborate lie to make themselves look better. We all lie to get ourselves out of trouble every once in a while. Those lies include little white lies and the grandiose ones that can get out of hand. However, we rarely lie to get ourselves into trouble. Generally speaking, we do it to make ourselves look better, not worse, not exiled, stoned, or martyred.

However, every single one of the apostles died for their faith. Paul was beheaded, Peter was crucified, and John died in exile. They were all cast out from their people, ostracized from other Jews, and tortured, their lives ruined by this story. If it was a lie, it had devastating consequences, and it's hard to believe anyone would stick to such a story if they knew their lives were on the line.

Many were painfully tortured. In Senator John McCain's criticisms of waterboarding as torture, he said it was not effective because people lie in order to make it stop. Lying to stop torture makes sense, but lying to continue torture or to be martyred does not. At any moment, the disciples could have said, "I made it up," and saved their lives. Yet none of them did. They were so profoundly changed by these experiences that they risked everything to share and uphold the story.

The final piece of evidence I considered was how Jesus grew in influence after his death. In my reading, I found at least five major public figures who were killed or crucified by the Romans in the first century, yet none of them developed a following after their death. Two of these individuals are spoken of in Acts 5. A leader named Gamaliel stood at a council meeting and said, "This has already happened twice. Two men, named Theudas and Judas the Galilean, claimed to be the Messiah. They gathered followers, too, but once the Romans arrested them and put them to death, no more came of it. The same will be true of this Jesus. If his following is just something men have made up, it will fail, but if it's from God, it will succeed."

Although Jesus was not the only one killed by the Romans, he would be the only one to remain in the forefront of our minds and lives. His influence did not die when he did. On the contrary, it only increased, ultimately changing the face of Western civilization. His resurrection altered the course of history and those who lived it.

A myth won't change you. A legend won't change you. A living savior with a body will change you—and if you believe that, you can transform hopelessness into a hope that cannot be extinguished. It can't be extinguished by loneliness, pain, or suffering. It's the kind of hope that always finds life in the midst of death—even in funeral homes, where you cry your eyes out without a care about who sees it, without having to fake it, because you genuinely can't imagine your life without this loved one. You find hope there because you believe in a true resurrection, where you will see this person again, and you don't have to fake that either.

I came to believe in that more fully than I ever had before because I pressed into that doubt to find my truth. I came to believe that the resurrection gave me the confidence that I need to know that nothing I do is in vain—everyone we see is eternal, they have dignity, they have value, and they can spend eternity with their Lord. I came to believe that every action we take moves us either toward or away from the Lord, and that nothing is in vain because Jesus is raised from the dead. I came to believe that I would see my brother again someday.

The gospel often sounds too good to be true, but if it weren't true, it wouldn't be so good. We don't need another bedtime story—something that makes you feel good whether it's true or not. No matter how much we love comedies, the world we live in often feels like a tragedy. We in America are very insulated from the fact of death—that everyone you love will die, and the only thing that may keep you from witnessing their death is your own. We don't like to think about that; instead, we tell ourselves stories to forget it. Many of us live messy lives, and we need hope. The resurrection can give us that hope.[2]

---

2   For further study on the resurrection I strongly recommend, "Surprised by Hope" by N.T. Wright and "The Reason for God", by Timothy Keller.

CHAPTER V

Still Alive and Still Proving It

———————●———————

"But he laid his right hand on me, saying, 'Fear not, I am the first and the last, and the living one. I died, and behold I am alive forevermore, and I have the keys of Death and Hades.'"

—REVELATION 1:17–18

AS A COLLEGE MINISTER, students often set up meetings with me to talk about their issues, faith, questions, and lives. Some often set up meetings just to sit down with a preacher, which is what I thought one woman was doing when she called me. For meetings with students, there were three places around campus I chose for meetings: the bakery, where we could talk casually if we did not mind those around us being able to hear it; the cafeteria, where people couldn't really hear, but plenty were within earshot; and a porch, where we were seen all over campus, but no one was close enough to hear.

As the woman and I walked toward the bakery, I asked how she was doing. She said she had been up all night crying, so I changed course to the cafeteria. She said, "Remember that e-mail from last semester?" I didn't, but to move the conversation along, I said, "Yes, how did that work out?" She replied, "I decided to have the abortion."

I altered our course to the porch, where we sat in view of others yet out of earshot. There, she told me her story, and I spoke to her about forgiveness, grace, and hope. She was overwhelmed with guilt and shame. Near the end of our conversation, she said, "I know no one is ever going to want me again. I'm damaged goods."

I started telling her about the resurrection. Paul in 1 Corinthians says anybody in Christ is a new creation, that the old is gone: "If anyone is in Christ, he is a new creation. The old is gone and the new has come." I said to the woman, "You're brand new." Those words steered her down a path toward healing. She sat through many more counseling appointments and shed tears, but she was energized by hope and the belief that she was brand new. For people with real problems, this simple sentence gives so much hope.

We do not have to wait until death to enjoy the benefits of the resurrection. It affects us here and now.

Years ago, in an article in a national magazine, a couple who spent their lives working with terminally ill children admitted that they told each of the patients that they were going to heaven. They said they weren't sure if it was true or not but that it seemed to help—that the patients felt better when they said it. Even those with only vague inklings of religious sentiment understand that this matters.

The resurrection is not just a good story we tell people hoping it makes them feel better. It is true, and the final reason I believe it is that I see a living Christ demonstrating his power every day. To paraphrase Acts 1, he is still proving to us in many ways that he is actually alive.

I have had the honor of witnessing a lot of incredible transformations in the church. A few years ago, a woman who desperately wanted a baby said a doctor had recently given her a grim prognosis—that the chances of her getting pregnant were slim to none. Still, she wanted fertility treatments, despite their exorbitant costs and uncertain results. The week before her first appointment was scheduled, she asked us to pray for her. She was anointed and prayed for as tears streamed down her cheeks. The following week, she was given a routine pregnancy test—something that had to be done before a patient starts taking hormones—and the nurses reported that she was pregnant.

Around the same time, a young couple brought their daughter to church. They were worried because she was well over two years old and had yet to start walking. They tried everything: expensive MRIs to check her brain and physical therapy to test her limbs and muscles. Doctors couldn't give them a reason why the little girl wasn't walking, so the couple asked us to anoint and pray for her. Two days later, while he was out of town, the father received a call from the physical therapist, who said she had bad news. He thought, *Oh crap, the insurance isn't going to pay for this*. But he kept that to himself and asked what she meant. The therapist said, "You're going to have to be a more attentive parent because your daughter is walking all over the place!"

Jesus shows up in small and big ways every day, healing people, emotionally and physically. He heals marriages and those who go through divorces with the same amount of love and grace. He heals those who feel so low and unwanted they don't think there's any way out.

That was the case for a man I'll call James. Over breakfast one day, James told me that when he was two years old, he witnessed his father murdering his mother. She was beaten to death with a hammer, and little James was taken by the court and placed in eight foster homes over the next four years, where he was routinely abused, harassed, and shamed. Every night of his life, James wet the bed, and every morning he was shamed for it. One foster family threatened him, but when he couldn't stop, they escalated their harassment: they wrapped the soiled sheet around his neck and forced him to sit outside at the bus stop, where his peers mocked him. One person hung a sign around his neck that declared, "I wet the bed." Finally, James was placed back into institutionalized care, where a psychologist pronounced that he would never be socially fit or well-adjusted. They said he would never be able to live and function in society.

Years later, a couple wanted to adopt a child but were too old for a baby. Case workers warned them that older children waiting for adoption often developed deep emotional issues, but the couple would not be dissuaded. They were given a book with more than five hundred pictures, and in it, they saw a picture of James. They pointed to him and said, "We want him."

That first day, they took him to a Chinese restaurant. James saw everyone around him eating with sticks. Never in his life had he seen a pair of chopsticks—this was only the second time he had eaten in a restaurant. He thought to himself, *I have to eat with sticks. If I don't, they are not going to want me as their son.* He grasped a chopstick in each hand and plunged the ends into the soup, splashing it all over the man who was supposed to be his new father. James thought, *I'm done. They don't want me. They're going to send me back. They're going to send me back.* He cried.

The man, covered in soup, reached under the table, where he had placed a toy boat—one he carved from balsa wood as a gift for his new boy. He handed it to James and asked, "Would you like to be my son?"

The couple took him home that night and tucked him into a bed with brand-new Roy Rogers sheets. James looked at the woman who would be his mother and said, "I wet the bed every night. I'm going to soil these sheets." She said, "Honey, if you do, we'll get up and wash them. But you're still going to be my son."

He never wet the bed again. And James is now a full-grown man, who, the day after our breakfast, stood in front of a church full of a thousand people and preached the gospel. No one in that room would have said he was socially awkward or unable to function in society. He was healthy, whole, and complete. He was living proof that Jesus is alive and at work healing people.

Sometimes, Jesus heals people through unexpected fertility; other times, he uses adoption. He does not often do what we ask or expect, but he is at work. We can trust him.

In 2007, James Cameron, director of the top-grossing films *Titanic* and *Avatar*, announced that he had found the lost tomb of Jesus. On National Geographic TV, he unveiled a sarcophagus that he had found. On the sarcophagus was the engraving, "Here lies Jesus, the son of Mary and Joseph." He declared that the "supposedly resurrected" body of Jesus had been found.

People thought that the Christian faith might crumble. Students came to ask me about it, and my initial response was that it couldn't be the real Jesus—dead people don't do the kind of healing that I have seen Jesus do. Archaeologists have since criticized the findings, and although it made for great television, it did not change the fact that the resurrection is not just a historic event—it is our present-day reality, and joy waits for those who press into this belief.

How? We have to ask ourselves if it's really something you believe in and why. We must take time to examine our faith because it is more than just a bedtime story. I want us to press into our belief in the resurrection. I want us to have a faith that's life-changing, healing, and hope-giving. I want us to believe in a God who made an actual person get out of an actual grave because I want our actual lives to be actually changed. I want us to have the hope that there is a living God who will change our lives now and forever. I want this for us, but not just because I believe and that belief has changed me from the inside out. I want this for us because we all deserve to feel such hope. That's why I wrote this book and relay the stories that have been shared with me over the years—because you deserve hope and the joy of an embrace from the living God.

God's Children or His Pets?

———————•———————

"For by grace you have been saved through faith. And this is not your own doing; it is the gift of God, not a result of works, so that no one may boast. For we are his workmanship, created in Christ Jesus for good works, which God prepared beforehand, that we should walk in them."

—EPHESIANS 2:8–10

IT'S SURPRISING HOW OFTEN I hear people referencing the film *Saving Private Ryan* when they talk about their faith. The film, set in World War II, follows eight soldiers under the guidance of Captain Miller as they go behind enemy lines to save Private James Ryan. Ryan's two brothers were killed in combat, and most of the men who save him also perish in the film. As Captain Miller dies, he says, "James, earn this. Earn it." Years later, when Ryan visits Miller's grave, he says, "I've tried to live my life the best that I could. I hope that was enough. I hope that at least in your eyes I've earned what all of you have done for me."

When Miller says, "Earn this," he's essentially saying, "We all died to save you," and urging him to lead a good life—almost on behalf of them. That's inspiring, but it can also be a tremendous load of guilt to bear, and it seems Ryan understands this, judging by what he says to Miller's grave: I've tried my best. I hope that was enough. After the war, the private goes back to life on the farm. I don't know about you, but if I were him, I'd be thinking, *I've got to plow really hard if I'm going to earn the deaths of so many men and the loss of my brothers.*

We tend to do that with Jesus—feel like we're supposed to earn it. He made an infinite sacrifice for us, and instead of interpreting that as his immense and vast love for us, we interpret it as a load of guilt, which becomes a burden. That's one of many misunderstandings in the church: the feeling that God doesn't like someone until he decides to have faith, believe, and repent—basically, until he has earned it. That's unfortunately the experience of so many. Instead of removing our guilt, the gospel makes us feel worse, it overwhelms with guilt, and people live their lives trying to feel worthy of God's love. Many of us have come to think that the best thing that could have happened would have been if we had died the day we first believed in Christ. We think, *On that day I knew he loved me, but ever since then, I have done nothing but disappoint him.*

If God has removed every obstacle between him and us so that we could experience his joy, why don't we feel it more often? Why does the Christian life feel like a treadmill instead of a spiral of joy? To put it simply, we are still trying to earn his love instead of enjoying it. We believe his opinion of us is based upon our behavior instead of our identity.

We mix up justification with sanctification

Imagine a young man gets his own bank account and starts writing checks. A thousand dollars here, two thousand dollars there—eventually, he has twenty thousand dollars' worth of debt. The bills start flooding in, and the bank fines him a thousand dollars for the overdrawn checks. The boy walks into the bank, sits down, and cries. A banker comes up and asks him what's wrong. When the boy tells him what happened, the banker says, "You're making a scene. If you leave the bank now, I will waive all the fines." That's all fine and well, but the boy is still twenty thousand dollars in the red. That seems to be how many view God: the banker gets us back down to zero so we can pay off that debt and start over. God forgives our sins up until this point, and from here on out, we have to be on our best behavior. Any mistakes we make henceforth show that we don't really love God, and we begin digging ourselves into debt all over again.

But what the gospel teaches us is that the banker doesn't simply forgive or waive our fines. The banker loves us so much that he marries us. The banker marries us, and all of our debt becomes his debt, all of his riches become our riches. Everything he owns becomes ours. That's what God has done, what he means when he said, "God made him who knew no sin to be sin for us that we might become the righteousness of God" (1 Corinthians 5). When he looks on us, he sees his own son, in whom he is well pleased, and he is delighted in us. He takes joy in us, even—and sometimes especially—when we screw up. Of course, we're going to screw up. Even on our best days, we make mistakes.

Romans 5:8 says, "God shows his love for us in that while we were still sinners Christ died for us." Nowhere in the Bible is there anything about "earning" the sacrifice that Christ made for us, and nowhere is there anything about "earning" God's love for us. The plain truth of the matter is, God loves us, and his love for us is like the love you have for a child— entirely removed from obedience. We are not his pets; we're his children.

Gracie was the greatest dog in the world—house-broken at six weeks old, and always obedient, happy to see me, and well-behaved. Gracie never tore into the furniture, never left messes around the house, and was so mellow I could bring her to theology classes at the seminary.

My kids were another story. They left messes wherever they went and constantly disobeyed me. As newborns, they did what newborns do: woke me up in the middle of the night with shrieks and cries. Whenever they wanted something—to eat, to be changed, or to be held—they yelled and hollered until someone came running. My wife—bless her crazy heart—used to ask me to babysit. It's sweet that she would think I was responsible enough for that. One afternoon, I was working at home and largely ignoring the kids, who were walking back and forth between the bathroom and their bedroom. I heard water running and thought nothing of it, but for good measure, I called out, "Hey, are you all playing in the water?" They said, "No, Dad," so I left them alone.

Finally, I got up from my desk to go check on them, only to find the most horrific mess: they had dipped sponges in a toilet that had not been flushed, and walked the soaked sponges through the hallway and into their bedroom, where they painted their sheets. The sheets changed colors when they were wet, and the kids were there, jumping around and playing in "pee-pee water," having just blatantly lied to me about what they were doing.

My dog never did that—my dog never made a mess like that and lied to me about it. And yet, when my dog became sick, I asked the vet how much it would cost to treat her versus the cost to put her down. I would never ask that question about my children. If my children were sick, there would be no question that they would get the best and most extensive treatments my wife and I could afford. Every penny I have earned since they were born has gone into raising them. My opinion of them—and my love for them—does not waver based on their obedience or their ability to follow my requests. My love for them doesn't need to be earned. It's inherent.

In the same way, God sees us as his children and loves us— no matter what messes we make of our lives, and no matter how many lies we tell and whom we tell them to, he loves us all the same. He is never disappointed in us; he only sees us through eyes of love, pride, and joy. He rejoices over us with gladness, he quiets us with his love, and he exults over us with loud singing (~~Zechariah~~ 3:17).

Zephaniah

Imagine you come home from a long, hard day of work and your children help clean up after dinner but really make a bigger mess in the process: the dishes are stacked irregularly in the dishwasher with clumps of food on them, so you have to take them out, rinse them off, and rearrange them. The crumbs that were on the counter were wiped onto the floor, so you have to sweep and mop after they go to bed. It might have been easier if you had done it all yourself, but instead of being mad at them, you are so thankful that they tried. You say nothing about the clumps of food or the arrangement of the dishes, the crumbs on the floor, or all the cleaning you're going to do after they go to bed. You only say, "Thank you." You love them for it. That's the way God receives our work. He is so thankful that we are trying. He doesn't need anything from us. If he wanted it done perfectly, he could probably do it himself. However, because he loves us, he lets us take part in it, and he delights in our participation.

At a conference, a man who was teaching asked a woman attending the seminars if she understood these concepts. He asked, "Do you feel like you're getting it?" She said, "I think so." She paused before adding, "This is really hard for me—the idea that God delights in me. It's hard for me because when I was a little girl, my dad was really harsh, but I loved him. I wanted so badly to get his approval that once, when my sisters and I were doing chores, I tried helping them hang his shirts on the clothesline, but because I wasn't tall enough to reach it, I grabbed one of the shirts and hung it up from the wheelbarrow. I was so excited to show him that I grabbed his hand when he got home and pulled him over to it, saying, 'See this, Dad? See what I did?' He took the shirt off the wheelbarrow, and there were two big rust stains where I'd clipped it. He saw those and yelled at me, saying, 'You ruined my shirt! Why did you do that? Why can't you do what you're supposed to? Why did you have to go and ruin this shirt?' I felt terrible, and what you're telling me, as I understand it, is that if God is my father, he'd look at me and say, 'You ruined my shirt, but I love you anyway.'"

The teacher said, "Not quite. In this situation, if God were your father, he would take the shirt off the wheelbarrow, immediately put it on, and give you a huge hug for helping him. He would wear that shirt to work the next day, and whenever anyone asked him about the stains, he'd say, 'My daughter did that. Isn't that awesome? See how much she loves me?'" [3]

That perfectly illustrates the misconceptions we have about God's feelings toward us, and how simple and beautiful his love for us actually is. We could stop seeing our sins as something so monstrous and unforgivable, and start seeing them as a kind of sickness. Everyone gets sick at one point or another, and everyone takes steps to heal themselves or their loved ones. In Jesus's lifetime, he was asked why he spent so much time with sinners. He replied, "The healthy do not need a physician, only the sick do." When a child is sick, we don't yell at her for not being able to go to school. Instead, we feel compassion toward her. Remember when you were sick as a child, and your mom comforted you? She helped you into clean pajamas, cuddled with you, cooked your favorite meals, and let you watch TV all day. Funny how those sick days became some of our fondest memories.

---

3   "Sonship" by World Harvest Mission.

Our weakest moments bring out the tenderness of others, not their disappointment. The same is true between us and God: he views our sins as something he can help us heal, it engages his pity, and he wants to nurse us back to health.

I remember well the days when my children would ask to go outside and play in the rain, and playing in the rain quickly became playing in the mud. I loved watching through the window as they splashed around, wrestled, and made mud patties. When it came time to come back inside, I met them at the door. They would try to clean themselves off, but everything they touched just got dirtier and dirtier. I didn't even want them to touch the water hose because I knew I would have to wash that. I would just say, "Stand still, and let me cleanse you." We are all still muddy children. All we can do is stand still, and let God cleanse us.

A child's weakness stimulates his parents' love and gentleness not their disgust. Do these parents look like they are ready to trade this child in for a healthy one? Of course not. God views our sin as sickness. He pities his sick children, and gives himself to heal them. Do you believe God feels this way about you?

CHAPTER VII

How We Make the Story Our Story

---•---

"They replied, 'We want to perform God's works, too. What should we do?'
Jesus told them, 'This is the only work God wants from you: Believe in the one he has sent.'"

—JOHN 6:28–29

"How do I get that goodness in me?"
—BRIAN REGAN, "POP TARTS", *I WALKED ON THE MOON*

"FAITH" IS A WILDLY OVERUSED WORD, so much so that it has taken on a kind of mystical quality. If you watch Monday Night Football, you might see someone holding up a sign that says "We Believe." When the Christmas season strikes, we see the word "believe" everywhere. Believe in what? Santa Claus?

What we've come to believe in is that faith itself holds a sort of power, and that power does something for us. "Just believe and good things will happen." It's important to question what we believe in and why because your faith is only as helpful as what you have faith in. And it can be destructive—a shopping addict believes the next thing will make her happy, and an alcoholic believes the next drink will set him right. In order to find life, we have to figure out what it is we really believe in, and where we place our faith.

Now that you see all that God has done to bring you into his spiral of joy, you must be asking, "How do I join that embrace?" The answer is, by faith. Unfortunately, that word has been so abused that it now causes more questions than it answers.

When I was in high school, I worked as a lifeguard. It was my dream job. I imagined I would be hanging out by the pool with beautiful girls in bikinis, but the reality was much, much less glamorous: weird tan lines, the stench of chlorine and sunscreen, and long days spent under the hot son. The only girls were a bunch of eleven- and twelve-year-olds. Pamela Anderson never walked in. Mostly, I just sat there for hours on end, feeling like a babysitter.

At night, the pool hosted private parties, which was the only time I ever had to save anyone. Strangely enough, the same thing happened three times, with three separate families and instances. Each time, a young mom would swim out to the deep end and coax her child to jump off the diving board. Her four- or five-year-old would stand there, scared, as she held out her arms and said, "Jump to me." Finally, the kid would jump into those eleven-foot waters, launching himself straight onto the mother's face. The mom would take a huge gulp of water and panic—the child wrapped around her head, both of them flailing and drowning. Each time, I dived into the water, and treading a few feet from each of them, said to the child, "Swim to me." The kid would release his hold on the mother, swim to me, and grab hold. Each time, I pulled him to safety.

That embrace is what's important—that embrace represents faith. I saved the child from drowning; he believed in me, but I did the work. Before that, he trusted that his mother would save him, but when they started pulling each other down, it was clear that that faith could drown them both. He didn't have to trust me in that moment, but he did. What I'm trying to communicate with the gospel is that you are putting your faith in the Son of God—he's the one who can save you. It isn't the power of your faith that matters; it's the fact that you have it and placed it in the right hands.

Faith is about letting go. In Chapter 2, we discussed that feeling of emptiness and relentless search for fulfillment and peace in all the wrong places. Like a child holding on to his drowning mother, we grasp tighter and tighter onto what fails us. Each time the child's mother would go down into the water, the kid pushed himself up off her, only pushing her down even farther, both of them sinking. In the same way, we look to success, our parents' opinion of us, our relationships, or our material things to fill this emptiness—we try to prop ourselves up on it and only end up sinking more.

Jesus comes to us and says, "If you want life, embrace me. Let me be the one thing who fills you. Let my love fill your emptiness. Let my pride in you become your self-worth. Stop pushing yourself up on things that are sinking. Instead, relax in my embrace, and let me take you home."

Faith is an act of letting go of the ineffective things you embrace and attaching yourself to the one person who can give you life. He is the one who does the work—he is the one who saves. And once we embrace Christ and place our faith in him, we stop fearing that our faith is not enough. The strength of it—the amount of it—does not matter. It may make your ride smoother, but it is not the power of your faith that saves you, but where you place it. Even if you have only a few ounces to spare and not swimming pools–full, Jesus will still pull you to safety.

There is a verse about how, even if your faith is the size of a mustard seed, you can still move mountains. It is supposed to comfort us by showing that even those of us with weak faith can be saved. Yet most people beat themselves up thinking, *I can't move mountains, so my faith isn't even the size of a mustard seed*. It's the opposite of what the text is trying to teach—that all you need is that tiny little seed.

Imagine there's a frozen river in the dead of a harsh Minnesota winter. A man starts to cross the river but doesn't know if it's strong enough to carry him. So he takes off his backpack and pushes it along the ice. He gets down on all fours and spreads his weight evenly. He's terrified, every step—or crawl—of the way. He imagines himself and his pack sinking into the cold waters and never coming up again. As he does, he hears an unbelievable noise—the clanking of bells, chains, and the rustle of animals. A wagon pulled by four horses passes by him, and the driver barely bats an eye. The man realizes that if the ice is thick enough to hold a horse, or four horses, it certainly isn't going to break under the weight of him and his pack.

Let me ask you this: Which man got across the ice? They both did. It was not the strength of their faith that mattered; rather, it was the strength of the ice. It doesn't matter whether his faith in the ice holding him was strong or not. He still got out there and was held. It wasn't his faith that was important; it was the ice, and his leaning into it. It's not just knowing that the ice is strong enough to hold you, and not just believing that the ice would, but actually getting onto the ice.

We have to trust in Christ to fill the void and deliver us from our sins and guilt. We have to make that commitment—in the same way the man commits to crossing the ice, and the same way the child commits to jumping into a stranger's arms to be saved. When we can release our grasp on what currently ails us and embrace Christ, we rest in his arms, embraced, and he is strong enough to bring us home.

One summer, my wife and I took our two oldest boys—who were very young at the time—floating down a lazy river in inner tubes. They were too small to have their own and too small for any of the life jackets available at this particular, so they had to ride in our laps. This would have been fine, except the lazy river was not nearly as lazy as anticipated or advertised. At one point, we went through a pretty rough rapid—one of those you see from far off and just dread going through. My son and I went through first, bobbing through the waves. As our tube sped out into calmer waters, I turned to see my wife and son hit a rock and flip over into the water. She held on to him for dear life, and because her arms were wrapped tight around him, she couldn't keep herself from hitting her head, scraping her elbows, and bruising her knees. Thankfully, they came up out of the water in one piece.

I steered us over to the shallows, parked my son and our tube on the banks, and went to retrieve theirs. Harold, our son, approached me with wide eyes and half a smile, shouting, "That was fun!" I laughed and said, "I bet you were scared, weren't you?" He said, "Not really. I made it because I held on to Mom."

It's sweet, but it's a kind of half-truth: Harold made it safely not because he held on to his mother, but because his mother held on to him. Life is a long ride. Sometimes, it feels easy, mundane, and even lazy. Other times, you sail through rough rapids you couldn't see coming, feeling terrified and coming out the other side covered in bruises. We will make it out not because our faith in Christ is strong, but because Christ is holding strongly on to us.

CHAPTER VIII

Feeding the New Reality

———————————•———————————

That's what it's like with all our dreams and our nightmares, Martin, we've got to keep feeding them for them to stay alive.

—JOHN NASH (PLAYED BY RUSSELL CROWE)

IN THE FILM *A BEAUTIFUL MIND*

"And now, just as you accepted Christ Jesus as your Lord, you must continue to follow him. Let your roots grow down into him, and let your lives be built on him. Then your faith will grow strong in the truth you were taught, and you will over-flow with thankfulness."

—COLOSSIANS 2:6–7

RECENTLY, a psychologist impersonating a nutritionist conducted a study on the power of belief. She created a milkshake that was three hundred calories but bottled it with two separate labels. On one label, the shake was called "Delite," listed at ninety calories and included low-calorie ingredients. The other, named "Indulge," was listed at 790 calories and claimed to include heavy cream, sugar, and eggs. They were the same milkshake, but given to two separate groups of people as two very different products. At the end of the trial period, when participants relayed their experiences, the group who drank the "low-calorie" smoothie said they were hungry sooner, and the chemicals in their bodies—the ones that tell us when it's time to eat—responded faster. However, the people who thought they were drinking a 790 calorie milkshake said they felt full, and their body chemistry confirmed that feeling. The first group not only thought they were hungry faster, but their bodies also believed it.[4]

What we believe is clearly integral to our emotional and physical health.

We all believe all kinds of things—right across the spectrum. One person believes Republicans are better for the nation, while another believes Democrats are better. We believe

4 *Mind over Milkshake: How Thoughts Fool Your Stomach.* Health News from NPR, April 24, 2014.

our kids are going to the best school, that our university was the best, or that our football team is invincible. We believe summer is the best season because we can swim, or winter is the best season because we can ski. Some beliefs are easily swayed, and some are so deeply ingrained that we take them to our graves. Some have far-reaching consequences, while others really don't. Some affect us deeply, but others have no real effect at all. But the good news is, you have the power to change your core beliefs.

Are you skeptical about this book so far? Or worse, are you discouraged? You may say you believe all of this but have never experienced anything like a spiral of love and joy. OK, my advice to you is to first make sure you are believing in the right message, and then feed that belief until it becomes the foundation of everything else you believe.

If we believe that Jesus's salvation is based on his faithfulness to us—as opposed to our faithfulness to him—then that can affect our day-to-day actions or how we feel about ourselves. It can bring us contentment and joy, whereas if we believe the opposite, we might walk around feeling overwhelmed, burdened, and guilty. The thing is, this belief can't just be one more on a long list of beliefs, in between "I believe so-and-so is the best presidential candidate" and "I believe my football team is the best." We need to believe on a deep level, right down to our soul, and that starts with ensuring we believe the gospel.

We need to sincerely sit down and ask ourselves, "Do I believe that Jesus died for my sins? Do I believe he is proud of me, has accepted me, and is delighted with me? Do I believe that more than anything else, he wants to bring me into his father's presence?" If we believe it, we should feel it—in the form of contentment, peace, and joy, as promised in the Bible. If you don't feel it, there are three reasons I can think of: (1) Jesus could be wrong and coming to him may not bring you joy, (2) you don't actually believe his message, or (3) the faith you believe in is not what he preached.

Let's set that first option aside because I've given my reasons for believing that Jesus is who the Bible says he is earlier on in the book, and if you are feeling skeptical, you may consult some of the resources located in the back of this book. The second possibility is very common: many don't believe his message, in the same way I never deeply and truly believed in the resurrection until my brother passed away. Maybe you don't believe the gospel, or maybe you have never been given room to doubt your faith. We all need to stop and ask ourselves, "Do I really believe the gospel, or do I just say that I do because of how I was raised? Does my faith belong to me or to someone else?" More often than not, we believe the messages we've been given but haven't been given the space to question whether that's the true gospel.

The American gospel goes something like this: "Work hard, need no one, be independent, be a good person, and reap the rewards of your own hard work." It's a message that made our nation strong but hasn't given an individual peace. Instead, we're led to believe that we are not enough—and when we are weak, we are never told that it's OK, that there is no shame in failure. The American gospel does not say, "God delights in his weak children as they are."

A fellow pastor approached me, feeling discouraged about his faith, and I asked him if he ever spoke to Jesus. When he said, "Yes," I asked, "How does he sound? What does he say?" The man said, "I hear things like 'Buck up, don't be weak. Do this by yourself, you don't need help. If you can't do this, you're a failure.'" I said that sounded more like a drill sergeant than the voice of Jesus.

The Son of God says, "Come lay down and find rest, bring your failures, your sin and shame, and I will welcome you." He also says, "You are mine, and I am proud of you."

Until we stop believing that the gospel is hard work, we will never find rest. When we believe the right message, then and there alone will we find rest and peace—the kind that comes from being in the presence of someone who is delighted with you.

Once we have confirmed that we are believing the right message, we must feed that belief and starve all the beliefs that compete with it. If we continue to feed outdated beliefs that do not serve us, we will continue to feel the emptiness and disappointment. We all have competing beliefs. I believe that the Lord of the universe loves me, and I also believe that I'm ten pounds overweight and so my wife finds me unattractive. I also believe my savings account is my primary security in life. Mostly I believe other people do not want me around unless I can make them laugh. The question is, which of these beliefs do I feed?

In the film *A Beautiful Mind*, a man has delusions of other people around him—imaginary people with whom he is close. Finally, he makes a decision to never talk to them again and enter into society, where he cultivates relationships with actual people. At Princeton, one of his new, real friends asks if he still sees his imaginary ones. He says, "I still see things that are not here. I just choose not to acknowledge them. Like a diet of the mind, I just choose not to indulge certain appetites."

We all have competing realities. We play one movie reel in our minds while the other movie reel plays right in front of our eyes. There's the way you imagine yourself and the way you actually move through the world. There are the day-dreams and fantasies you have during the day and the dreams you have at night and the real, tangible waking state. There are the people who live around you, and the world you're actually in, with all of its beauty and despair. The question is, which reality do you feed?

A seventh-grade girl once met with her pastor because she felt depressed and suffered from low self-worth. Her parents wanted her to seek counseling, so she sat down for a session with the pastor. In the middle of him talking to her about the gospel and how Jesus loves her, she interrupted him, saying, "I know all this, but what does it matter if Jesus loves me when none of the boys in the seventh grade will look at me?"[5]

We all know that feeling, right? What good is it that Jesus loves me if I can't pay my rent, find a job, find someone to love me, fix my marriage, help my family, and so on? What this girl was feeding was the reality that her value—her joy—depended on having a boyfriend, on being popular, on having people like her, on being appreciated for her looks—an unfortunate by-product of popular culture's messaging. She fed that reality instead of the reality that she said she believed. She said, "I know all this." She knew that the maker of heaven and earth had a personal interest in her, that he actually loved her, and that he was invested in her. If she fed that belief, really meditated on that, then the likes or dislikes

---

5   Tim Keller uses this illustration in many sermons.

of the seventh-grade boys would fade into the background. Although it's hard to see it as a seventh grader, we all know as adults how little we recall the details of our time in the seventh grade. The little things start to matter a lot less. That's not to discount how she felt, but when we put things in the larger context of our life, it helps us shift our focus.

Even though we may have left seventh grade behind, many of us still carry the same insecurities. We desperately want approval, from others or from ourselves. One professional I know still arrives at work every day at 6:00 a.m. to win the approval of his father, and his father died more than a decade ago. We just can't feel good about ourselves unless someone we care about approves of us. I have found that my self-esteem often depends upon the opinion of the person I value most. Not one of us can really do anything to change the opinion of another person. However, we can change whose opinion *we* value most. The world is not very impressed with me, but the Lord of the universe thinks I am precious. He loves me so much that he gave his own son for me. I choose to spend my energy making his opinion the one I value most.

How does that work in day-to-day life?

Once, a friend of mine missed out on a huge contract because he sent his proposal in too early. The secretary he delivered it to laid it aside and forgot to include it when she collected all of the applications to hand in to the chief executive officer. When he told me about it, I said, "Isn't it good to know your well-being depends on the Lord of the universe, who loves you so much he gave his son for you, and not on the mistakes of a bad secretary?" Often, even I forget this—living in an imaginary, kind of schizophrenic world, where my well-being depends on how much money I make, how good I look, and on the whims of those around me. This is the imaginary world we live in: one in which our well-being depends on only us. But in the actual world we live in, the Lord of the universe has loved me so much that he gave his own son for me. Not even a hair can fall from my head apart from his permission. I need to be reminded of that. We all do.

And we all need to get out of the schizophrenic world to be reminded of reality—to regain our sanity and feed our souls. How do we do that? How do we feed our faith? Two key ways, for me, have always been worship and community. Worship is what we do in church each week, and where I go to restore my sanity. Hearing the gospel once isn't enough. It can be too hard to believe, too good to be true, or too difficult to override the patterns of thought that we have so deeply ingrained in us. So, we need to be reminded week after week, and every time I worship that God is on his throne and that he has received me into his family. He promises to walk beside me, day in and day out.

That idea is somewhat a reversal of how many people think, as the skeptics and cynics want to say that church tells us about a fake world, another reality. What I'm teaching is that this is the real world. A world where people say that the destiny of humanity depends on the next presidential election is not real—it's silly, and there's nothing real about it.

It helps to have people close to us who understand—a solid community. For me, I've always found a strong sense of community at the places where I worship. In college, I found most of my friends at church, and it seemed easy to meet people there, where we had something in common. Sometimes, though, the church makes this hard. We feel afraid to let people know who we really are, and we put on masks, pretending everything is fine in order to avoid rejection. The problem with masks is people can only love the mask they see, and the more they love the mask you put on, the more alone you can feel—and the more you tell yourself "If they truly knew me, they would reject me." Building a community on the backs of a falsity makes us feel like imposters—lonely, rejected, ashamed, and afraid.

What we need is to seek communities that let us be ourselves. Let us admit to our weaknesses, doubts, anxieties, fears, and faults. Only then are we able to feel the love offered to us, and only then will we believe that people love us for ourselves. And if we have a community of people who love and support us—despite and because of our weaknesses and shortcomings—we will be able to strengthen and accept the belief that God loves us as well, failure or not.

Four years to the day after my brother died, my sister passed away. What were the odds of that? At her funeral, I felt eerily similar to the way I had four years earlier, standing by my brother's freshly dug grave. The same thoughts washed over me, and as person after person arrived to comfort me, I realized I would never be able to maintain a belief in the resurrection on my own. I needed a community—people around me who could remind me that the world I see or the world I watch in my head are not the only worlds that exist.

If our faith is well-fed and we are full of belief, we need to make that the lens through which we interpret our lives. In this way, we see our circumstances in light of God's love, instead of interpreting his affection for us according to our exterior circumstances. For instance, if we get sick and our first thought is, "I'm sick because God's angry at me" or "I'm weak, and God will see that I'm worthless," then we're going to feel even worse about feeling sick. Often people think things like, *So-and-so left me because there's something wrong with me.* That only adds more shame and despair to what are already poor circumstances. And the Bible teaches us to view our circumstances through what we already know about God.

Roman 8:32 says, "He who did not spare his own son but freely gave him up for us all, how will he not with him, give us all things?" There is so much in this life that we do not know: we can't know what will happen tomorrow or next year, what we're going to be like, whether we're ever going to get past the struggles we experience now, or whether we will have a whole new list of struggles. What we do know is this: God loves us so much that he gave his own son for us. Whatever has come to us has come from the hands of someone who loves us.

With that in mind, we can shift our thinking from "I lost my job because God is mad at me" to "The Lord loves me so much he gave his own son for me, and he has decided I don't need this job anymore. I may not see the reason now, but I may someday, and there must be something else out there for me." Now, that doesn't mean we have to paint smiles on our faces and pretend everything is fine. People often think that to be a good Christian you have to be happy and cheerful all the time, even if it means faking it. Faith is deeper than fake smiles. Faith says, "Even if I walk through something as terrible as death itself, I know the Lord loves me, and I know he's going to walk through this with me. He brought light to the world through the death of his son so he could bring light to us through these events. I know he is not going to abandon me or leave me hanging here alone."

If we want our faith in the gospel to change us—to bring us peace and rest—then we have to feed our faith that Jesus delights in us. We have to retire the old patterns that aren't doing us any good. We have to feed that faith to the detriment of those false beliefs—beliefs such as we are only worthy if we succeed or if other people love us. Those things we believed will not give us life but instead take life from us. They ultimately set us up for failure.

What we ultimately want to do with the gospel is heal deep problems. The comedian Russell Brand once said, "Heroin isn't my problem. Deep fear and alienation are my problem." There are the surface problems and then there are the deeper roots of the problems. If someone's an addict, at some level they do have to address the surface problems, because they may not be capable of taking on reality. But to continue with this example, the way the gospel heals addiction and self-destructive patterns is by helping us feel like we are not going through this alone. These issues arise in part because we are separated from God, and we are trying to fill that void—running away from him in many cases. Coming back to God through the church ideally gives us a community of people to support us, and we would also have God there with us. You won't feel the need to anesthetize yourself from that alienation if you believe—seriously, deeply believe—that you are not alone. And the best way to remind ourselves of all this is to worship at church, what the Bible calls the body of Christ—a visible reminder of what he is like on earth.

One Sunday, a young mother invited me to her home after church so I could speak with her eight- and ten-year-old daughters. When I arrived, I asked what they wanted to talk to me about. The ten-year-old spoke first. "Why doesn't God always answer our prayers?" I stepped lightly, knowing we were on sacred ground, and asked what she meant. She said, "Well, we've been praying every night for our dad to come home. He came in last night and told us he was never coming back home, that he was leaving our mom. Why didn't God answer all of those prayers?"

It's a question people ask often: if God is listening, why didn't he hear me when I said I wanted things to work out this way?

These girls grew up attending our church, so I answered the girl's question with one of my own, one I thought she may have heard me talk about in church that same day, "Did Jesus always get what he asked for when he prayed?"

She shook her head and said, "No."

I asked, "When did he not get his prayers answered?"

She said, "He asked to not have to go to the cross, but God

made him go there anyway." I nodded, but before I could say anything, she added, "You know, God brought something good out of that. He brought salvation and light and hope out of that unanswered prayer. Maybe he can bring something good out of this."

I smiled and said, "I think you're right, and I think he can."

CHAPTER IX

Of Campouts and Christmas Mornings

———————•———————

We can go back home. . . for the first time!

—THE CAPTAIN, *WALL-E*

"Now all glory to God, who is able to keep you from falling away and will bring you with great joy into his glorious presence without a single fault. All glory to him who alone is God, our Savior through Jesus Christ our Lord."

—JUDE 1:24

MARGARET WAS A SWEET, eccentric woman who attended our church with her husband, the church's custodian. When we first started, we rented a space in a public school where we could all meet, and the school assigned us Margaret's husband as our custodian. The first Sunday we met there, she came with him and sat in the front row, and each week she returned to claim her seat. She was so faithful in her attendance that we asked if she wanted to join the church. When she said yes, the two of us agreed on a time to meet so I could interview her and understand her reasons for attending. Over lunch, she told me about her faith and belief in God's grace. At the end, I said, "I would love for you to join the church. Are there any questions you have for me?"

She said, "How are you going to minister to me while I'm dying?"

It was a big question, and one I wasn't expecting. I asked if she thought she was dying. Yes, she said, she thought she was. She said she had been ill for a long time, was only getting sicker, and didn't believe she had much time left.

I asked, "Are you afraid?"

She said, "I'm terrified."

"Well," I said, "Margaret, I'm going to take you to Jesus so you don't have to be afraid, and I will surround you with community so that you don't have to be alone. That's what I'm going to give you. I hope that's enough."

She said, "That's the best that I can hope for."

Margaret did not die soon as she had thought. She lived in our community for the next eight years, becoming an integral part of the church. When we moved to our own building, she came with us, making the church lobby her home away from home. When people entered the church, she treated them like travelers who were coming home. Eventually, Margaret's health declined. It was around Christmas when she was admitted to the hospital. When I went to visit, she said, "I need you to keep your promise to me." She didn't need to remind me of what that was. When everyone left the room so we could talk, I asked if she thought she was dying. Yes, she said. I asked what she wanted me to say at her funeral, and how we could best take care of her family when she was gone. We talked about the peace of the gospel, and what it would be like to see Jesus. Up until that day and that conversation, Margaret was agitated and anxious. Her husband said she wouldn't let him out of her sight, but at that point, she began to find peace.

When Margaret died in the hospital, she was surrounded by friends. She died with no fear. She was at peace. That kind of death is the best any of us can possibly hope for—falling asleep at peace and well-loved.

We really do not like to talk about death. Even in hospitals, we stay away from the topic like it is the plague. If you bring up death, you often are made to feel like a villain. But whether we talk about it or not, every one of us will face it. So let's spend this last chapter talking about how God's spiral of joy will carry us through the last trial—death.

There are two sentiments I hear from almost everyone I speak to: a fear of death and a fear of what comes after death. In our modern world, we often deal with the first fear by pretending like we aren't going to die and choosing not to think about it. Traditionally, pastors were the ones who comforted people in a world filled with death—back when people died in their homes and half of all pregnancies resulted in death. Today, with our advances in modern medicine, death is rare, and it's easy for us to forget about it altogether. Now, pastors aren't just comforting people grieving deaths but also reminding them that we are all going to die, and this life is temporary. The fear of what comes next raises a lot of questions: Will we really face the judge? What will it be like when we see him?

For the believer, dying will feel like going to sleep and waking up at home.

When we were living in Mississippi, my boys asked me to take them camping. It was the middle of the week and sixty-five degrees, so I agreed, saying that we'd go that weekend. The funny thing about Mississippi weather, especially in winter, is that it can be warm one weekend and freezing the next. Of course, that weekend the temperature dropped to seventeen degrees. The ground was frozen, and the air was miserably cold, but my boys were so excited that I couldn't bring myself to break the promise I'd made. We drove out to the campground where I immediately lit a fire. We played around it for a while, then cooked hot dogs and made s'mores. We stayed by the logs and flames as long as we could. When it got dark, and the temperature dropped even more, we climbed into the tent, where the boys wrestled, and we took turns telling stories.

We settled down to sleep. However, there were four of us and only three sleeping bags. I thought it would be okay, and that it might even be sweet to share a sleeping bag with my four-year-old son—not only sweet but practical. I thought, *He'll feel safe and won't be afraid, and I'll be warm because I'll have a little heater next to me.* Everyone cozied up and fell asleep. I quickly realized that sharing a sleeping bag meant I wouldn't be able to move. I couldn't turn over all night. I was stuck sleeping on the cold, hard ground on one side. I awoke with a terrible pain. It felt like I'd had a stroke. I couldn't move my right arm or right leg. Awake, cold, in pain, and miserable, and not knowing what to do, I wondered how was I going to get through the rest of the night. I laid there, listening to the cold wind whistle through the thin fabric of the tent and wanted to whisper, "Hey, guys, are you all miserable, too?" However, the boys were all dead asleep, apparently quite comfortable.

I thought, *All right, get out of the tent, and make a plan.* I climbed into the van to clear my head. It was so cold in there I started to freeze. I turned on the ignition to warm up, and the clock on the dashboard lit up: 9:45. The night hadn't even started yet! There was no way I was going to be able to stay in the tent all night.

I swiftly made up my mind. I left the heater running in the van, crept back to the tent, and without waking up the boys, lifted them back into the van one by one. I drove home, carried each of them into the house, and tucked them into their beds. There was enough time left in the evening to watch television with my wife, and I was in my own warm, comfortable bed by ten thirty.

The next morning, after I awoke, I went to the kitchen and started making pancakes. The boys came in as they usually did on Saturday mornings, having slept in and needing to slowly shake off the extra hours of sleep. One by one, each of them had this sudden realization, and their faces lit up:

"Wait a minute. We went camping last night, fell asleep in a tent, and woke up at home!"

The victory over death is so complete that the New Testament never actually says that a Christian dies, only that they go to sleep. What my boys experienced is akin to the picture of a Christian and what we have to look forward to: falling asleep in an earthly tent, in a hard, cold world, and waking up in our Father's warm home, where he welcomes us. When we awake, we will enjoy a place of healing. Revelation paints a picture of life after death like waking up in a spa with huge pools and hot tubs, restful and calming, where Jesus welcomes us to stay and heal, but adding that we shouldn't wait too long because he's created this entirely new, beautiful world for us that he wants us to start enjoying. We emerge with new, glorified bodies to enjoy this world after it's been renewed and rebuilt for us. We enjoy our relationship in him with him.

Revelation 21 says, "There's no need of a sun there, for God is there." We will be in his presence, face-to-face with him. We'll be strong enough to behold his glory. We'll be right in front of him, before him, the way his son has lived before him for all of eternity. For the very first time, we will actually see with our own eyes the smile for which we have been longing.

Unfortunately, many Christians are afraid of the very idea of what judgment day is going to be like. They picture fire and brimstone. That fear indicates that they still don't quite believe that God loves them and is on their side. I believe it is more biblical to see judgment day like Christmas—specifically, the first Christmas I bought a present for my mom. I was in fourth grade, the youngest of the family, and I was tired of just drawing pictures for my mom while the rest of my siblings bought her gifts. However, there were a few things getting in my way of actually buying her something nice: I didn't have any money, I didn't have any way to go to a store on my own, I didn't actually know what she wanted, and I didn't know how to wrap a Christmas present. Not knowing how to get around all those obstacles, I resorted to moping and sulking around the house. My mother noticed and asked if something was wrong. I told her something about not being able to buy Christmas presents for people, and she nodded, filing that information away for later.

That week, she looked out the window and said, "Look at all these sticks in the yard. I sure wish somebody would move them. I'd pay ten dollars for somebody to move these sticks." I hurried outside and collected all the sticks, which was my responsibility anyway, as part of my weekly chores. Just this once, my mother paid me for it, and after the yard was clean and I was thanked and given ten dollars, she said, "I'm going to the store to do a little shopping. Would you like to come?"

Of course I did. On the way there, she mentioned she'd seen some necklaces and wished she could have one.

The necklaces were nine dollars. I picked one out, brought it up to the counter, paid for it, and put it in a bag. As soon as we got home, I raced back into my bedroom and started wrapping. The only box I could find was huge, and I tore through an entire roll of wrapping paper—no matter which way I cut it, it didn't fit. I started crying and brought the box out to my mother. She wrapped it for me, making it look easy, and I placed it under the tree.

Christmas finally came. I went to the Christmas tree to retrieve the present that my mother had paid for, picked out, drove me to get, and wrapped. My mother unwrapped the box she had wrapped, clasped the necklace around her neck, and hugged me in what felt like the biggest hug in the history of hugs. She said, "I love it. Thank you so much. It was just what I wanted." She was so delighted to see how much I wanted to give her a gift, and I was so delighted to see her so pleased. She was overjoyed to see me happy, and both of us were caught in that spiral of delight once again.

That is what judgment day is going to be like for us: we're going to bring all of our good works to our Father, and he's going to remember every one of them—every glass of water we gave to a child in his name, every single good intention we ever had. And he's going to embrace us in an enormous hug and thank us. Thank us! Even though he was the one who made all of the sacrifices to bring us into his presence, he will thank us. That is how delighted he is in us.

First, let us lay down what we think is going to fulfill us, and stop living in a wretched spiral of shame. Lay that down and embrace the love that will fill you. Faith is the embrace, and repentance is the letting go. It may not sound like enough, and sure, maybe the good works we bring to our Father on judgment day amount to very little—maybe they are crap compared to our sin. But he has paid for all of it. He is that good, and he loves us so much, that he's going to throw his arms around us, embrace us, and say, "Thank you. It's just what I wanted. I love it." Finally, we will feel how we were created to feel, how Jesus saved us to feel: the glory of God, his smile, and his embrace.

About the Author

RICKY JONES is an epic failure who has continually fallen backwards into grace. He grew up a true redneck in rural West Tennessee and left the woods to attend Vanderbilt University with no idea what he was getting into. While there he met the gospel of grace through Reformed University Fellowship, and his wife Bianca.

They planted RiverOaks Presbyterian Church in Tulsa, Oklahoma, in 2006. He and Bianca have four teenage boys, all of whom are above average. Ricky passionately believes the church should be like Jesus: a place of grace and rest. He also believes no one can thrive alone, and no one should try.